Meditations on the Pentateuch

Scripture and Illustration

Sandra Enders

The forty-five illustrations by Julius Schnorr von Carolsfeld are reprinted here with approval from Dover Publications. The original engravings were published in his *Die Bibel in Bildern* (The Bible in Pictures) at Leipzig, Germany between 1852 and 1860.

ISBN# 9780692148815

Printed in the United States of America

Amazon Create Space - Kindle Direct Publishing

First Edition

Dedication

To Dad, who was always there for me. May we meet again one day!

CONTENTS

Preface

This writing came together as an afterthought to my *Meditations on the Rosary: Scripture, Psalms, Illustration, Guided Imagery* published in 2017. Growing up as a Roman Catholic, the Old Testament was never stressed. In fact, I recall asking my parents as a small child, what Jewish meant, and they looked at each other and avoided answering the question. They were not well read, aside from the New Testament Bible, and often avoided answering inquisitive questions in general. It wasn't until the past twenty years that I became interested in the Old Testament. I am intrigued with the Dead Sea Scrolls, the origin of the angels, and energy psychology. My spirituality has expanded beyond Catholicism, although I could never leave the Church.

I believe there are higher intelligences out there that we can connect with through cognitive focus, prayer, meditation, and mindfulness practices, a cosmic consciousness as some call it. And I do not feel that one must choose between Creationism, Evolutionism, or Intelligent Design, because all three have merit to some extent. I teach sociology and psychology at secular colleges and it annoys me that every textbook I have used has always included a few paragraphs on Darwin's Natural Selection theory, usually in the chapter on how empirical scientific research is done in the social and behavioral sciences. And that is fine, but I need to add in that there are two other huge theories that carry some weight. For just a moment, take the God-spiritual-belief aspect out of the thought process and just use common sense and reasoning. Do you really believe that we began walking upright as bipedal hominids *over five million years ago* through natural selection, but yet, the homo-sapien hits the scene on Earth only *fifty thousand years ago* and we are already flying to the moon and mars? And creating non-biological artificial intelligence? And genetically altering DNA without natural selection? And the scientific community tells us that this is all being done through nothing more than Darwinian Natural Selection? I think not!

There has been outside intervention with the development of man all along we just have not discovered exactly what it is, and we may never. The human brain development has accelerated tremendously since the Enlightenment period and the emergence of the scientific method. It is a phenomenal process of discovery, I admit, but it excludes metaphysical phenomena that man cannot yet explain through our current observational sensory perception abilities. And so, it is brushed off as pseudoscience, if that!

My pastor, Father Jeremiah Murasso, who often preaches on the decline and decay of American culture, proposed a question during a homily in the fall of 2017. He asked the parish; *what was the pivotal day that began the decline of belief or need for God in our society*? I thought about that question for months. My first instinct was 9-11, but then I thought further, it is far bigger than the disputes with the Muslim Fundamentalists, in fact I can understand their anger at American society (although it does not justify the violence). And it is also much bigger than the progressive political liberalism that infiltrated the country over the past century, because let's face it, both sides have arguable merit. And then I thought about Nietzsche with his *God is dead* comment first appearing in his 1882 collection, *The Gay Science*. That of course led to the flow of academic thought that argued, *science was the new god*, and the liberalism that continues on our American campuses today. All shrouded in their empirical evidence, their logic, and peer review process!

My answer to Father Murasso, is that it may have been November 24th 1859, the day that Charles Darwin's *On the Origin of Species* was released. The theory of evolution was in the air throughout the Western intellectual centers at that time, and I don't dispute it was coming. I also don't dispute it is an excellent evolutionary theory, the natural mutation due to the need for biological organisms to adapt and survive their immediate environment. I just don't think it is the *only mechanism* at play in the evolution of man. Even his colleague, Alfred Russel Wallace, argued that there was something else going on concerning the intellect, consciousness, and morality in the human that was not in any other animal.

Just ask yourself, how is human invention and innovation, artistic and creative pursuits, the desire to learn, and for scientific discovery, a biological need for survival? How did we move from simple survival to development of artificial intelligence through the process of only natural selection, and in such a short period of time?

In his 1905 biography *My Life*, Wallace posited that *"there is a difference in kind, intellectually and morally, between man and other animals; and that while his body was undoubtedly developed by the continuous modification of some ancestral animal form, some different agency, analogous to that which first produced organic life, and then originated consciousness, came into play in order to develop the higher intellectual and spiritual nature of man".* However, Darwin had the formal education. Darwin had the means and money to get his theory published. *On the Origin of Species* sold out of printed copies the first day out. *That was the pivotal day, that day in 1859, when God began the descent in society.* It is Darwin's theory that ended up in every textbook on every campus across America. And Wallace is now just a footnote for academics to consider. I often wonder what might have happened had it been the reverse. Had not Wallace's theory taken hold, might have we held on to the mystique of God? Of the need for God? Could we have held on to the belief that elusiveness is merely a characteristic of Him, and that phenomenon does not need to be observed or be replicated to be true, as science tells us?

My heart has always been in Christian teachings and although I disagree with some areas of Catholicism, I am familiar and very comfortable with its rituals, teachings, and social good works that it promotes, so I could never see myself leaving it. I am not a theologian, this book is not a cited scholarly writing, and I did not use formal literary biblical criticism. It is merely my personal way of delving into the first five books, so I can learn more, as a Christian, where it all began. The narration is intertwined with scriptural verses to initiate and encourage personal insight, reflection, and direction.

This book takes the reader through the Pentateuch using over one hundred passages of scripture and forty-five illustrations from Julius Schnorr von Carolsfeld, a German Lutheran illustrator of the mid-19th century. It includes some light narrative on the various topics throughout, which frankly has no specific format. I chose topics that interested me and let the spirit move me.

Chapter one, *In the Beginning,* looks at the early years of the Hebrew speaking people and how Judaism began. Most scholars claim that the first five books were written down approximately 600-400 BC, so it was oral tradition for about 1000 years from the time of Moses, and another 200-500 years before that for the earlier beginnings of Abraham. The creation and flood story, I consider myth, as most ancient cultures around the world used similar stories to explain their world and origins. The chapter covers some basic terminology and texts of Judaism, nothing at all in depth.

Chapter two looks at the first book, the Book of Genesis, which is divided into three major areas and broken into fifty chapters based on subject matter. The Creation (1:1-2:3) covers the Creation story, considered myth as far as literary forms go. The Primeval History (2:4-11:26) covers the flood story of Noah, considered myth or legend. The Patriarchal History (11:27-50:26) covers the history of the patriarchs and can be considered myth, legend, or historical documentation depending on the interpretation, although myth and legend often evolve out of real events and oral tradition.

Chapter three covers the second book, the Book of Exodus, and maintains four sections broken into forty chapters. The book begins with the Prologue (1-2), then moves to God's Deliverance of Israel (3-18), the Covenant at Sinai (19-24), and lastly, God's Royal Tent in Israel (25-40). The writings tell about Moses' flight from Egypt and the journey of his people through the dessert, aided by God. Most important in the book is the revelation of God to Moses and the covenant made between them. Moses disseminates God's requests to the people which later becomes Mosaic Law in the history of the Hebrew people.

Chapter four looks at the third book, the Book of Leviticus, which includes six sections and is split into twenty-seven chapters. Much of this book reiterates again from the Book of Exodus, God's words to Moses on Mount Sinai. Instructions are given that emphasize ritual, legal, and moral practices rather than beliefs. It begins with the Five Main Offerings (1-7), the Installation and Ministry of Aaron and His Sons (8-10), the Distinction Between Clean and Unclean (11-15), the Annual Day of Atonement (16), Holy Living (17-26), and it ends with the Regulations for Offerings Vowed to the Lord (27).

Chapter five covers the third book, the Book of Numbers, which includes five sections and thirty-six chapters. It begins at Mount Sinai where the covenant is made between God and Moses, Israel at Sinai Preparing to Depart the Promised Land (1:1-10:10), the Journey from Sinai to Kadesh (10:11-12:16), Israel at Kadesh Delay Resulting from Rebellion (13:1-20:13), the Journey from Kadesh to the Plains of Moab (20:14-22:1), Israel on the Plains of Moab Taking Promised Land and Appendixes are combined (22:2-36). The book includes two censuses taken of all males able to bear arms from twenty years and up, thus the name Numbers. The first is done at the beginning of the journey at Mount Sinai. The second census is done on the plains of Moab. There the land gets divided and the twelve tribes begin to become distinguished separately.

Chapter six covers the fifth and last book, the Book of Deuteronomy which has five sections and is broken into thirty-four chapters. A Preamble (1:1-5) begins the book, following is an Historical Prologue (1:6-4:43), Stipulations of the Covenant (4:44-26:19), Ratification; Curses and Blessings (27-30), and lastly is the Leadership Succession under the Covenant (31-34). Similar to Leviticus, this book also reiterates from the Book of Exodus, God's words to Moses on Mount Sinai. Instructions are again given, however rather than the focus on strictly ritual, legal, and moral practices, here the focus of the law and practices is on faith, belief, and God's love.

All Scriptural verses used in this writing were taken from the New American Bible Revised Edition (NABRE 4th). The 1st edition of the New American Bible (NAB) was first published in 1970 stemming from the Confraternity of Christian Doctrine (CCD) initiated in response to Pope Pius XII's *Divino afflante Spiritu* encyclical in 1943 which called for new translations of the Bible from the original languages, instead of the Latin. The CCD met from 1941 to 1969 and resulted in the NAB and the move away from the Latin translation. This change coincided with the liturgical principles and reforms of the Second Vatican Council (1962-1965). A revised 2nd edition (RNAB) was released in 1986, which is today the only translation currently approved for Mass in the Catholic dioceses of the United States and the Philippines. Traditional phraseology excluded from the 1970 edition was restored to the New Testament, reverting somewhat to the resemblance of the 1941 Confraternity version, as opposed to the 1970 NAB. The 3rd revised edition (RNAB) was published in 1991 with the Book of Psalms amended to expand on gender-neutral language. The 4th revised edition to the NABRE was released in 2011.

The work of the NAB originated out of the Vulgate, the fourth-century Latin translation that became the Catholic Church's official Latin version of the Bible during the 16th century, an outcome from the Council of Trent (1545-1563). Saint Jerome (347-420AD) is credited for the original translation of the Vulgate. He was commissioned by Pope Damasus to revise the *Vetus Latino*, which was an unorganized collection of Biblical texts written in Old Latin. The Vulgate was the first single consistent Latin text translated from the original tongues of Greek and Aramaic. By the 13th century the Vulgate had become the most commonly used version until the move to the New American Bible in the 20th century. The Nova Vulgata has been the official *Latin version* of the Bible for the Catholic Church since 1979 with origins in the Second Vatican Council coinciding with the revisions of the entire English version of the NAB.

The forty-five illustrations throughout the book are by Julius Schnorr von Carolsfeld from his *Die Bibel in Bildern*, German for *The Bible in Pictures*. This work, containing thirty parts, was published at Leipzig, Germany between 1852 and 1860. Schnorr was part of the Nazarene Movement, a subgroup of the Romanticism movement in art at that time. It was a move away from the then dominant Neoclassicalism art. The Nazarene movement focused on historical and biblical scenes with a mission to revive honesty and spirituality in Christian art. This group was one of the first to turn away from the academies teaching and salon art. Schnorr's biblical drawings were a prelude to many stained-glass window designs that later emerged in churches and cathedrals throughout Europe.

Schnorr was born in Leipzig, Germany in 1794. He was a Lutheran Christian, although held a broad non-sectarian view. He was the son of Veit Hanns Schnorr von Carolsfeld, a draughtsman, engraver and painter, from whom he received his initial artistic education. At seventeen he entered the Vienna Academy, and moved to Rome a few years later. There he was commissioned to decorate the entrance hall of the Deutsche Akademie Villa Massimo, a prestigious German institute in Rome, where he illustrated the works of the Italian poet Ariosto using frescoes. From Rome he moved back to Germany and focused on wall painting in Munich. Schnorr moved to Dresden to take a professor position at the academy there in 1846. Soon after he was appointed director of the Gemäldegalerie, an art museum in Berlin. Schnorr married Maria Heller, the stepdaughter of Ferdinand Olivier, another German artist. They had one son together, Ludwig Schnorr von Carolsfeld, an operatic tenor, who died at the age of twenty-nine. Schnorr died in Munich seven years later.

A list of all forty-five illustrations of Schnorr are included in Appendix I along with the scriptural caption notation, and all other scriptural passages throughout the book. Although nothing but scripture passages are cited, a list of references that were used in this writing, are listed at the end of the book.

Concerning the use of chronology and time designation, this book uses the traditional *BC* and *AD* system, with both following the year or century, but without the use of periods. The BC represents *before the birth of Christ*. AD, stands for *anno domini*, Latin for *in the year of the Lord*, referring specifically to the birth of Jesus Christ. The Gregorian Calendar, which is used here, begins using the birth of Jesus as the starting point with the year zero. It was instituted in 1582 by Pope Gregory XIII with the *Inter gravissimas* papal bull in February of 1582. It was intended to reform the Julian calendar which had been proposed by Julius Cesar and used since 46BC. In recent years, an alternative form of BC/AD has become popular, with *BCE* meaning *before common era* and *CE* meaning *common era*.

Acknowledgements

Many thanks to Christine Sandford, wife of Deacon Wayne Sandford. She has been my spiritual director, Small Christian Community Bible group leader, and Christian mentor for the past fifteen years. Chris dedicated her life to ministering and evangelizing the Word of God as Jesus Christ instructed us to do. By modeling her life as a true Christian, she has surely been an inspiration, positive role model, colleague, and friend to me!

I also what to thank all the beautiful people I met, worked with, prayed with, and broke bread with at the St. Clare Parish in East Haven CT. Unfortunately, the church was closed on June 26th 2017. We have since then become one body in Christ, a Roman Catholic community joined with two other parishes in the town (St. Vincent DePaul and Our Lady of Pompeii). So we now, being many people of diverse talents, time, and opportunities, trust in the Lord that this new union as St. Pio of Pietrelcina Parish, under the pastoral direction of Reverend Jeremiah Murasso, is as God has planned!

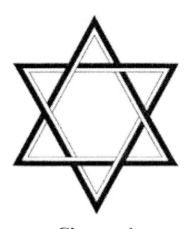

Chapter 1

In the Beginning

The Pew Research Center on Religion and Public Life maintains global data on religions of the world. In their 2010 census the center found that with the world close to a total of seven billion (6,895,890,000) in population, Christians lead the way with 31.5% and Muslims not far behind with 23.2%. The Pew Center estimates that by the middle of the 21st century, the total population of the world will be over nine billion and the two leading organized religions, Christian and Muslim, will be close in numbers with just under three billion each. This same 2010 census shows Hindus holding 15%, Buddhist 7.1%, with Folk Religion close to 6%. The unaffiliated fall to about 17% and Jewish are at a low of .2%. The projection for the unaffiliated in the United States are estimated to grow from about 16% of the total population in 2010 to 26% in 2050. The growth of Muslims and Christians will be driven by the expansion of the African population, a high-fertility region. Both groups are predicted to increase as a percentage of the global numbers and combined would make up more than two-thirds of the world's population by 2100 (69%), up from 61% in 2050 and 55% in 2010.

Revealed Religion:

Organized religion in the Western world tends to center around the three monotheistic religions, all of which are considered *revealed religions*. So, what does it mean to be a revealed religion? And what is that in contrast to? The answer is that revealed religion is known through divine revelation, arrived at through a metaphysical source, or from speaking directly to God. Faith is central to revealed religion and logic is not necessarily needed. The alternative is religion based on philosophical reasoning, such is more often found in the Eastern world, such as in Buddhism, Confucianism, Taoism, and Hinduism. This is not to say that religion cannot mix the two areas. For instance, Hinduism maintains many gods and faith has a wider meaning. Faith in a creator God is not central, however, faith in *the self* and its eternal existence is important. In contrast, there were many great figures through history that used reasoned arguments to defend Christian faith, a revealed religion. Thomas Aquinas and Anselm of Canterbury both wrote eloquent philosophical writings that argued for the existence of God. Aquinas's was cosmologically based on the origin of the universe and Anselm's was ontologically based related to the nature of being. So, organized religions do mix both faith and revelation with philosophically reasoned arguments.

Judaism is considered the first documented revealed religion in the world, with teachings delivered directly from divine sources, rather than through man's philosophical logic and reasoning. Although Adam and Noah supposedly conversed with God, Abraham is generally considered the father of Judaism with God's promise of land in Canaan. Abraham is also considered the father of the two other major revealed religions that arose from the same origins. The three religions, Judaism, Christianity, and Muslim are all considered Abrahamic religions and honor the same God. Jesus Christ is believed by Christians to be totally divine and totally human. He preached God's word in the form of Christian philosophy about 30AD. This was documented in the New Testament. Then God later revealed himself to Mohammad in 610AD which was recorded in the Quran (Koran).

Early Monotheism:

Most people understand the difference between monotheism and polytheism, the belief in one god verses the belief in multiple gods. But the move from many gods to one god took place over time. *Henotheism* is the belief in only one god, however acknowledges the existence of other gods of equal validity that can be worshiped. In Henotheism the choice of which god is often determined by various factors, such as cultural, historical, geographical, or sometimes for political purposes. Conversion from one god to another is possible if necessity arises. *Monolatrism* is the belief in the existence of many Gods, but the worship of only one God. However, monolatrism denies that other gods are worthy of worship. Scholarly consensus is that both forms of religious worship were early stages to monotheism and evidenced in Biblical scripture. In the Book of Exodus, the gods of the Egyptians are mentioned.

[11] Pharaoh, in turn, summoned the wise men and the sorcerers, and they also, the magicians of Egypt, did the same thing by their magic arts. [12] Each one threw down his staff, and they turned into serpents. But Aaron's staff swallowed their staffs. (Exodus 7:11-12)

[12] For on this same night I will go through Egypt, striking down every firstborn in the land, human being and beast alike, and executing judgment on all the gods of Egypt—I, the Lord! (Exodus 12:12)

[3] You shall not have other gods beside me. (Exodus 20:3)

Monotheism was practiced in principle in ancient Israel, but most scholars believe that it did not become strictly enforced until after the Babylonian exile in the 6th century BC. Prior to that time, the Israelite God, Yahweh, had competition with various other gods and cults from the surrounding cultures. These pagan gods were collectively referred to as Baals by the Hebrews, which was a general generic term, although early Hebrew texts makes use of the term with their own God, Yahweh, as well as used in reference to other deities. Traditionally the term insinuated a god related to the Earth, solar gods, or patron deities, although recently are thought to have been specifically associated with the storm and fertility god, *Hadad*. The later use of Hadad was taken into Christianity and Islam and used disparagingly under the guise of *Beelzebub*, who was considered a demon. *The point is that terminology and meanings change over time and depend on context and culture.* The movement from polytheism to monotheism was not done suddenly. It was a very gradual progression over centuries. The move to henotheism occurred about the 8th to 7th century BC, then moved to monolatrism through the 7th to 6th century BC before strict adherence to monotheism began after the Babylonian exile.

Holy Texts:

Christian scholars usually refer to the first five books of the Old Testament as the *Pentateuch,* a Greek word meaning *five scrolls.* Jewish scholars, however refer to these texts as the *Torah.* Although some may refer to the Torah as being the complete Hebrew Bible, it is only the first of three sections. The term Pentateuch came out of Hellenistic Judaism, a form of Judaism in the ancient world that combined Jewish religious tradition with Greek culture. Alexandria and Antioch were points of convergence and text translation during the period of 323BC (death of Alexander the Great) and 31BC (emergence of Roman Empire). The cultural changes during this period were extensive through the region, which influenced later riffs within the Hebrew population concerning divisions between the religious groups.

The *Septuagint* is considered the primary Greek translation from the original Hebrew and Aramaic. It is estimated that the translation took place during the 2nd to 3rd century BC. The Jewish scholars living in Alexandria translated the text using the Greek word *nomos, meaning norm doctrine, and law*. Greek and Latin Bibles then began the custom of calling the Pentateuch, the Law, since the Hebrews considered their religion their law.

The Torah, a Hebrew word meaning *instruction or law*, maintains the central teachings of Judaism, but the complete canonical collection of Jewish texts is referred to as *Tanakh*. It consists of twenty-four books and was used as the primary source for the Christian Old Testament. The word Torah though, sometimes can have a range of meanings, anywhere between the entire writings of the Hebrew texts, Jewish teachings, culture and practice, to the ancient texts or later rabbinic writings. However, the Torah is only the first five books of the Tanakh, which includes the complete compilation of Jewish teachings, the trials and tribulations of the Israelites, and specifically the relationship and Covenants made with their God of Israel. The teachings from the combined texts directly dictate a set of moral and religious obligations as well as civil laws. The term *Mikra*, is another Hebrew word for the Tanakh meaning *that which is read.*

One central theme of the writing consists of the origins of the Hebrew speaking people. The term *Hebrew is a language*, although it is often used to describe a people, a religion, or a culture. The Israelites were the Hebrew speaking Jewish and Samaritans who lived in the Canaan area. The language belongs to the West Semitic branch of the Afroasiatic linguistic family. It is the only living Canaanite language left, which declined in everyday use between 200AD and 400AD. Modern Hebrew is one of the two official languages of the State of Israel today, the other being Modern Arabic. Aramaic was also a widely spoken language during the antiquities era. It is from the same Semitic language family as Hebrew and Arabic but is rarely spoken today. Aramaic was the language that Jesus spoke.

Traditionally, the teachings maintained three divisions, *Torah* (Teaching), *Nevi'im* (Prophets), and *Ketuvim* (Writings). Tanakh was originally an acronym for the three sections (TaNaKh). The Torah includes the first five out of the twenty-four books and was originally called the Torah of Moses. It was passed down through oral tradition that Moses wrote the Torah, although many modern scholars doubt that is completely true. As mentioned earlier, the Christians call these first five books (Torah of Moses), the Pentateuch.

The *Nevi'im,* the second section of the Tanakh, consists of eight books of the prophets, and is divided into two groups, the Former Prophets and the Latter Prophets. The Former cover Joshua, Judges, Samuel and Kings. The Latter include the books of Isaiah, Jeremiah, Ezekiel and The Twelve minor prophets, which are considered one book.

The *Ketuvim* is the third and final section of the Tanakh and is sometimes called *Hagiographa.* The Ketuvim is believed to have been written from divine revelation, although with lower authority than prophetic. There is a total of eleven books in the Ketuvim which is split into three sections. The Three Poetic Books (*Sifrei Emet*), include; Tehillim (Psalms), Mishlei (Book of Proverbs), and Iyyobh (Book of Job). The Five Megillot (*Hamesh Megillot*), include; Song of Songs/Solomon (Shir Hashirim), Ruth, Lamentations (Eikhah), Ecclesiastes (Qoheleth), and Ester. The last section includes Daniel, Ezra, and Chronicles (Divrei ha-Yamim).

To put it in context in comparing the Christian Old Testament texts to the 24 books of the Tanakh, they are fairly similar in book order and inclusion. The Catholic Church includes 46 books, the Protestant groups use 39 books, and the Eastern Orthodox uses 51 books. The Muslim Quran/Koran however uses a very different format and is not split into Old and New Testament at all. It includes 114 chapters, or *Surah's* as the sections are called, 87 which are classified as *Meccan*, and 27 are *Medinan.*

The Muslim text is split into two major parts related to the *location of the revelation.* The complete text is told by Mohammad and was revealed directly from God. The chapters that occurred in Mecca, prior to the prophet's move to Medina (Hijrah) is termed *Meccan.* The writings revealed after that event is termed *Medinan.* The Meccan chapters generally deal with faith and scenes of the hereafter, while the Medinan chapters are more concerned with organizing the social and religious life of the Muslim worshipers and community. The chapters are arranged roughly in order of descending size and unlike the Tanakh and Bible are neither chronological nor thematic.

Babylonian Exile:

The Babylonian captivity lasted about seventy years, with variations of dates thought to be between 608BC to 516BC. This separation caused two strands of oral tradition and interpretation of God's message to eventually develop, which evolved into the Babylonian and Jerusalem version of the *Talmud*.

The Talmud is the central text of what eventually developed into current day Rabbinic Judaism. In most Jewish communities, prior to modernity (post Enlightenment), the Talmud was the center of Jewish culture and the foundation of Jewish thought and guide for living. Oral Torah was passed down through the generations until its contents were finally committed to writing following the destruction of the Second Temple in 70AD. The spread of Greek culture followed by Roman occupation also influenced divisive ideas on Jewish law and lifestyle.

Tradition holds that in the fifth century BC, Ezra was a scribe responsible with leading some of the Jews back to Jerusalem from Babylon after the exile. He is credited for writing The Book of Ezra, the tenth in the eleven of the Historical Books of the Old Testament. He is also thought to have developed the *Great Assembly* of elders. This organization was known to be the precursor to the Sanhedrin as the authority on Jewish religious law. The *Parashot* is the annual reading schedule in which the entire Torah can be read in one year. The Great Assembly divided the five books into 54-55 sections for reading on each Sabbath. Each individual section is called a Parashah or a Sidra. The readings from the liturgy is chanted publicly by a designated reader in Jewish prayer services. Each reading is named after the first word in the Hebrew text of the specific reading. The schedule follows an annual cycle beginning and ending on the Jewish holiday of Simchat Torah. The schedule is based on the lunisolar Hebrew calendar, rather than the Gregorian calendar based solely on the sun. This schedule is based on 54-55 readings, the exact number varying between leap years and regular years. At the start of each of the following five chapters the 54 sections are listed in Hebrew and English along with the coinciding chapter and verse of the Bible.

Essenes / Sadducees / Pharisees:

Three competing groups emerged during the 1st and 2nd century BC. The *Essenes* were the least in number of the three groups. Although some lived in the city, most congregated in rural communal settings. Their lifestyle was characterized by ascetic living, abstinence from worldly pleasures with the pursuit of spiritual goals. Their life often included poverty and celibacy, with a message and ritual practice toward mysticism, messianic, and apocalyptic ideas. Although the authorship of the Dead Sea Scrolls has been challenged, many give credit to the Essenes. The 972 manuscripts were found between 1946 and 1956 across eleven caves around the Dead Sea Qumran area, with another cave recently found in 2017.

The *Sadducee*s were active in Judea during the Second Temple Period, and often associated with an upper social and economic echelon of society. This group held political, social and religious roles, including maintaining the Temple. Their sect is believed to have disappeared over the 1st century AD, although speculated that it may have developed into a later Jewish group called the *Karaites* who held similar views as the Sadducees. The Karaites have historically rejected Oral Law, deriving their religious practice strictly from the Written Law. The Sadducees recognized only the Written Torah, rejecting doctrines such as Oral Torah.

The *Pharisees* were the strongest of the three groups, whose beliefs later became the foundation for Rabbinic Judaism. This group was a political, social, religious, and philosophical school of thought all in one. Their ideas conflicted with the Sadducees and division worsened with the Roman occupation. Besides religious views, cultural conflict also existed. The Sadducees favored Hellenization, the spread of Greek influence in the culture. The Pharisees resisted this enculturation and held firm to traditional Hebrew culture. Other liturgical and ritual areas of disagreement persisted, the importance of Mosaic Law, and differing interpretations of the Torah and how to apply it to Jewish life.

Rabbinic Judaism and the Talmud:

Rabbinic Judaism arose out of the Pharisee line and has been the mainstream form of Judaism since the 6th century AD. The books of the Tanakh were passed down through the generations and Rabbinic tradition maintains that the written be accompanied by an oral tradition. Most of this school of thought is based on the belief that the written laws from God to Moses at Mount Sinai was in addition to the oral traditions known as the *Mishnah*. This contrasted with the Sadducees and other groups, which did not recognize the oral law as divine authority, nor the Rabbinic interpretation of Jewish scripture. Rabban Yochanan ben Zakkai, a Jewish sage (*tannaim*) in the Second Temple period was a primary contributor to the core text of the Mishnah. His name is often preceded by the honorific title, *Rabban*. He is regarded as one of the most important Jewish figures of his time. He was the first Jewish sage attributed the title of rabbi in the Mishnah.

The term Talmud usually refers specifically to the Babylonian Talmud *(Talmud Bavli)*, written in the 6th century AD. But there is also an earlier collection known as the Jerusalem Talmud (*Talmud Yerushalmi*), written in the 4th and 5th century AD. The entire collection consists of 63 tractates and teachings of rabbis and Jewish scholars dating before the time of Christ through to the 5th century. It includes a variety of subjects including Jewish law (Halakha), ethics, philosophy, customs, history, folklore, etc.

The Talmud consists of a combination of oral law (Mishnah) and rabbinical analysis of the Mishnah, referred to as the *Gemara*. These authoritative writings, called *Masoretic Text*, were originally written in Aramaic and Hebrew. The text was later interpreted, copied, edited and distributed by a group of Jews known as the *Masoretes* between the 7th and 10th century AD. The two versions of the Gemara, as mentioned are the earlier version, the Jerusalem Talmud (Yerushalmi), compiled and published about 350–400AD by scholars in Tiberias and Caesarea. The Babylonian Talmud (Bavli), was compiled and published about 500AD by the scholars of Babylonia.

Talmud:

*combination of oral law (Mishnah)

*with rabbinical analysis of Mishnah (Gemara)

***Jerusalem Talmud (Yerushalmi) compiled about 350–400AD

***Babylonian Talmud (Bavli) compiled about 500AD

(also called *Masoretic Text*, originally written in Aramaic and Hebrew)

There are three distinct styles or genre of writing in the Talmud compiled during the first centuries AD. One is referred to as the *midrash*. The purpose of this genre was used to *resolve conflicts in deciphering difficult passages* of the text of the Hebrew Bible. The application of Rabbinic interpretation needed to stay in alignment with the earlier religious and ethical teachings. The second form of literature used is called *aggadah*, Aramaic for *tales* or *lore*. It consists of teachings of wisdom, stories, and parables. The aggadah tends toward mysticism and is sometimes used along with the Jewish Law. The Jewish Law referred to as *halakha*, is translated as *the way to behave*. It is derived from Written Law and Oral Law and is used to teach a principle or make a legal point.

As mentioned earlier, the Tanakh text is split into readings called the parashot, a system that began early in Judaism. This system continued for quite a few centuries with early Christianity. But eventually in the early 13th century an English Cardinal, Stephen Langton, once the Archbishop of Canterbury, created the chapters and verse system in the Bible that is still used today.

Chapter 2
The Book of Genesis
(Bereshit / In the Beginning)
12 Parashot / 50 Chapters

Parashah	Hebrew	English	Chapter/Line
1	Bereshit	In the beginning	Genesis 1:1-6:8
2	Noach	Noah	6:9-11:32
3	Lech-Lecha	Go forth yourself	12:1-17:27
4	Vayeira	And He appeared	18:1-22:24
5	Chayei Sarah	Life of Sarah	23:1-25:18
6	Toledot	Generations	25:19-28:9
7	Vayetze	And he went out	28:10-32:3
8	Vayishlach	And he sent	32:4-36:43
9	Vayeshev	And he settled	37:1-40:23
10	Miketz	At the end of	41:1-44:17
11	Vayigash	And he drew near	44:18-47:27
12	Vayechi	And he lived	47:28-50:26

***

The word Genesis is Greek in origin and comes from the word geneseos, which appears in the Septuagint, the pre-Christian Hebrew to Greek translation. Depending on the context that it is used in, the word can mean *birth, genealogy,* or *origin*. The Book of Genesis includes fifty chapters and twelve parashiot. It is generally divided into three major areas based on subject matter. The first section is the story of Creation. It offers the story of the world being created in six days by Elohim, a generic Hebrew term for God. The second section is the Primeval history which covers Adam and Eve, a second creation story where God is referred to as Yahweh, a more personal term for God. He creates all the world in one day. He also created Adam, the first man from dust, then God places the man in the Garden of Eden with a companion female named Eve. Everything was done in the same day. The story of Noah and the flood followed the Creation story. The last section is the Patriarchal history which looks at the history of the patriarchs; Abraham, Isaac, and Jacob. The Patriarchal Age is generally thought to be between 2100BC to 1800BC, which coincides with the middle of the Bronze Age period.

Genesis is the foundation for understanding the rest of the Bible. It includes the creation story, the great flood, genealogies, migrations of people, and geography of the area. But more importantly it speaks about relationships between people, highlighting the relationship between God and humankind. It stresses that there is only one God who is sovereign over all that exists and that He has unlimited freedom to overturn anything of human origin. It explains God's covenants with his chosen people of Israel. God pledges his love and faithfulness to them and asks that they promise theirs to him. It offers us the oldest and most profound statement of faith:

Then he believed in the Lord; and He reckoned it to him as righteousness. (Genesis 15:6)

I. The Creation (1:1-2:3)

The Creation text attempts to locate Eden, thought to be the area of origin of the homo-sapien, located in or near Mesopotamia. Much of the Book of Genesis reflects other early sources documented about ancient Mesopotamia. The area is situated between the Tigris and Euphrates River system in the Middle East. Today it primarily covers the area of Iraq and Kuwait, and some parts of Turkey, Syria and Iran. Although the early patriarchs later settled in Canaan, somewhat to the south-west, their original homeland was Mesopotamia where Abram was born. The first part of Genesis, chapters 1-38, is greatly influenced by Mesopotamian culture. The later part, chapters 39-50, portray somewhat of an Egyptian character.

The earliest written histories (3500-4000BC) outside of Judaism also verifies much of what is found in Genesis. The Sumerians and Akkadians, including the Assyrians and Babylonians, dominated the area at that time up to the fall of Babylon in 539 BC, when it was conquered by the Achaemenid Empire. It later fell to Alexander the Great in 332 BC, and after his death, it became part of the Greek Seleucid Empire. The issue of Greek influence on the Hebrew speaking people was of concern causing some divisiveness later in the various religious groups that formed. The Babylonian exile during the 7th century BC also had profound cultural influence.

[28] God blessed them and God said to them: Be fertile and multiply; fill the earth and subdue it. Have dominion over the fish of the sea, the birds of the air, and all the living things that crawl on the earth. [29] God also said: See, I give you every seed-bearing plant on all the earth and every tree that has seed-bearing fruit on it to be your food; [30] and to all the wild animals, all the birds of the air, and all the living creatures that crawl on the earth, I give all the green plants for food. And so it happened. [31] God looked at everything he had made, and found it very good. Evening came, and morning followed—the sixth day. (Genesis 1:28-31)

The First Day of Creation

By Julius Schnorr von Carolsfeld (Die Bibel in Bildern 1852-1860)

[1] *In the beginning, when God created the heavens and the earth,* [2] *and the earth was without form or shape, with darkness over the abyss and a mighty wind sweeping over the waters,* [3] *Then God said: Let there be light, and there was light.* [4] *God saw that the light was good. God then separated the light from the darkness.* [5] *God called the light "day," and the darkness he called "night." Evening came, and morning followed—the first day. (Genesis 1:1-5)*

The Second Day of Creation

By Julius Schnorr von Carolsfeld (Die Bibel in Bildern 1852-1860)

⁶ Then God said: Let there be a dome in the middle of the waters, to separate one body of water from the other. ⁷ God made the dome, and it separated the water below the dome from the water above the dome. And so, it happened. ⁸ God called the dome "sky." Evening came, and morning followed—the second day. (Genesis 1:6-8)

The Third Day of Creation

By Julius Schnorr von Carolsfeld (Die Bibel in Bildern 1852-1860)

⁹ Then God said: Let the water under the sky be gathered into a single basin, so that the dry land may appear. And so, it happened: the water under the sky was gathered into its basin, and the dry land appeared.¹⁰ God called the dry land "earth," and the basin of water he called "sea." God saw that it was good. ¹¹ Then God said: Let the earth bring forth vegetation: every kind of plant that bears seed and every kind of fruit tree on earth that bears fruit with its seed in it. And so, it happened: ¹² the earth brought forth vegetation: every kind of plant that bears seed and every kind of fruit tree that bears fruit with its seed in it. God saw that it was good. ¹³ Evening came, and morning followed—the third day. (Genesis 1:9-13)

The Fourth Day of Creation

By Julius Schnorr von Carolsfeld (Die Bibel in Bildern 1852-1860)

[14] Then God said: Let there be lights in the dome of the sky, to separate day from night. Let them mark the seasons, the days and the years, [15] and serve as lights in the dome of the sky, to illuminate the earth. And so, it happened: [16] God made the two great lights, the greater one to govern the day, and the lesser one to govern the night, and the stars. [17] God set them in the dome of the sky, to illuminate the earth, [18] to govern the day and the night, and to separate the light from the darkness. God saw that it was good. [19] Evening came, and morning followed—the fourth day. (Genesis 1:14-19)

Babylonian Cultural Influence:

The words Hebrew, Jewish, and Israelite are often used interchangeably to refer to the same group of people, although the three terms have slightly different meanings. The word Hebrew specifically describes an ancient language used by a group of people who inhabited the area around Mesopotamia or today's Iraq and Kuwait area, north-east of Israel. The Israelites were a branch of Hebrews who settled in Palestine (today's Israel) after 1200 BC. The Jewish people were another group who descended from the southern Israelites and settled in the Kingdom of Judah.

Most of the early Hebrews were nomadic pastoral people who inhabited lands between Mesopotamia and Egypt, but as the area began to prosper, cities developed, and some Hebrews settled in the region's cities. The Old Testament tells us that the patriarch Abraham came from the Sumerian city of Ur. He later migrated to northern Mesopotamia about 1850 BC. The Hebrew speaking people mingled with many other groups, sharing myths, gods, values, and customs. To the north there was Mesopotamia, and to the south was Egypt.

The Mesopotamian Hammarabbi Code had an influence on Jewish law. And the Hebrew creation myth and their account of Noah and the flood mimicked the Enuma Elis, which was the Babylonian creation myth. The Enuma Elis was discovered in 1849 at Nineveh (Mosul, Iraq). It was written in Akkadian, an extinct Semitic language spoken throughout ancient Mesopotamia. On clay tablets of Sumero-Akkadian cuneiform script, it portrays the early Mesopotamian culture. The tablets describe the creation of the world, a battle between gods focused on the supremacy of Marduk, the creation of man destined for the service of the Mesopotamian deities. The writing ends with a long passage praising Marduk. Later versions replace Marduk with the Assyrian primary god, Ashur. The dating of the Enuma Elis is not known but estimated anywhere between the 18th century BC and 7th century BC. The Mesopotamian culture greatly influenced the development of early Judaism.

The Fifth Day of Creation

By Julius Schnorr von Carolsfeld (Die Bibel in Bildern 1852-1860)

²⁰ Then God said: Let the water teem with an abundance of living creatures, and on the earth let birds fly beneath the dome of the sky. ²¹ God created the great sea monsters and all kinds of crawling living creatures with which the water teems, and all kinds of winged birds. God saw that it was good, ²² and God blessed them, saying: Be fertile, multiply, and fill the water of the seas; and let the birds multiply on the earth. ²³ Evening came, and morning followed—the fifth day. (Genesis 1:20-23)

The Sixth Day of Creation

By Julius Schnorr von Carolsfeld (Die Bibel in Bildern 1852-1860)

[24] *Then God said: Let the earth bring forth every kind of living creature: tame animals, crawling things, and every kind of wild animal. And so, it happened;* [25] *God made every kind of wild animal, every kind of tame animal, and every kind of thing that crawls on the ground. God saw that it was good.* [26] *Then God said: Let us make human beings in our image, after our likeness. Let them have dominion over the fish of the sea, the birds of the air, the tame animals, all the wild animals, and all the creatures that crawl on the earth.* [27] *God created mankind in his image; in the image of God he created them; male and female he created them. (Genesis 1:24-27)*

II. Primeval History (2:4-11:26)

The Primeval History covers the story of Adam and Eve in the Garden of Eden, the first two humans created by God. From the Adam and Eve story, the history moves onto the story of Noah and his family, the ark and flood story, and the Rainbow Covenant made between Noah, God, and all God's living creatures. This covenant is unique in the scriptures because it applies to all humanity, while the other covenants are mainly agreements made between God and his followers. Noah is the tenth generation from Adam. The Primeval History closes with the story of the Tower of Babel.

The Nephilim:

The race of *Nephilim* was described in detail in the *Book of Enoch*, an ancient Jewish religious text, whose credit is given to Enoch, the great-grandfather of Noah. The writings date between 300BC to 100BC and have surfaced again with the recent Dead Sea Scrolls. The book is not considered canonical, although was accepted at one time in the early Christian Church. The Jews in Christ's time was familiar with the book which honed a more mystical tone as with the Essenes group. It is often cited in angelology as being the origin of the angels. The story is briefly mentioned in Genesis chapter six.

¹ When human beings began to grow numerous on the earth and daughters were born to them, ² the sons of God saw how beautiful the daughters of humans were, and so they took for their wives whomever they pleased. ³ Then the Lord said: My spirit shall not remain in human beings forever, because they are only flesh. Their days shall comprise one hundred and twenty years. ⁴ The Nephilim appeared on earth in those days, as well as later, after the sons of God had intercourse with the daughters of human beings, who bore them sons. They were the heroes of old, the men of renown. (Genesis 6:1-4)

The Sabbath

By Julius Schnorr von Carolsfeld (Die Bibel in Bildern 1852-1860)

[2] And on the seventh day God ended His work which He had done, and He rested on the seventh day from all His work which He had done. [3] Then God blessed the seventh day and sanctified it, because in it He rested from all His work which God had created and made. (Genesis 2:2-3)

Suzerain Treaties and the Covenants:

The term covenant in a secular sense merely means a promise or a contract between two parties. The covenantor makes a promise to a covenantee to do (affirmative covenant) or not do some action (negative covenant). Covenants between God and his people are considered important in all three Abrahamic religions. There are two major types of covenants, the obligatory type and the promissory type. The obligatory covenant deals with the relationship between two parties of equal social status. In contrast, the promissory type of covenant focus on the relationship between two of unequal standing.

In the Ancient Near East, treaties referred to as suzerain-vassal treaties, were common. These treaties were often between kings, usually to honor each other's boundaries, to maintain trade relations, or to return run-away slaves. The greater king is the *suzerain* and the lesser king is a prince, or a lesser lord in the service of the greater king, considered the *vassal*. The lesser lord is considered a representative of all the common people who are under the protection of the greater king, and he is designated to enforce the treaty among the masses. These suzerain-vassal treaties included identification of both parties, all titles, and any history that the two parties may have had prior.

The contract illustrates to the vassal how much the suzerain has done to protect and establish the vassal who therefore owes obedience and allegiance to the suzerain. It also includes a list of stipulations concerning the requirements of the vassal in detail. The contract ends with blessings and curses of the suzerain, which depends on if the requirements have or have not been met. Both parties would keep copies of the treaty. A ceremony or ritual is then done to complete the oath and commitment. Animal sacrifice was common in the ending process of committal. Biblical covenants of the Pentateuch were patterned after the suzerain-vassal treaties of that time. Although God revealed himself to various figures in the Pentateuch, there were three covenants of major importance, with Noah, Abraham, and Moses.

The Fall of Man

By Julius Schnorr von Carolsfeld (Die Bibel in Bildern 1852-1860)

² And the woman said to the serpent, "We may eat the fruit of the trees of the garden; ³ but of the fruit of the tree which is in the midst of the garden, God has said, 'You shall not eat it, nor shall you touch it, lest you die.'" ⁴ Then the serpent said to the woman, "You will not surely die. ⁵ For God knows that in the day you eat of it your eyes will be opened, and you will be like God, knowing good and evil." ⁶ So when the woman saw that the tree was good for food, that it was pleasant to the eyes, and a tree desirable to make one wise, she took of its fruit and ate. She also gave to her husband with her, and he ate. ⁷ Then the eyes of both of them were opened, and they knew that they were naked; and they sewed fig leaves together and made themselves coverings. (Genesis 3:2-7)

The First Judgement of God

By Julius Schnorr von Carolsfeld (Die Bibel in Bildern 1852-1860)

[16] To the woman He said: "I will greatly multiply your sorrow and your conception; In pain you shall bring forth children; Your desire shall be for your husband, And he shall rule over you." [17] Then to Adam He said, "Because you have heeded the voice of your wife, and have eaten from the tree of which I commanded you, saying, 'You shall not eat of it': Cursed is the ground for your sake; In toil you shall eat of it, All the days of your life. [18] Both thorns and thistles it shall bring forth for you, and you shall eat the herb of the field. [19] In the sweat of your face you shall eat bread till you return to the round, for out of it you were taken; For dust you are, And to dust you shall return." (Genesis 3:16-19)

The Expulsion from Eden

By Julius Schnorr von Carolsfeld (Die Bibel in Bildern 1852-1860)

[22] Then the Lord God said, "Behold, the man has become like one of Us, to know good and evil. And now, lest he put out his hand and take also of the tree of life, and eat, and live forever" [23] therefore the Lord God sent him out of the garden of Eden to till the ground from which he was taken. [24] So He drove out the man; and He placed cherubim at the east of the garden of Eden, and a flaming sword which turned every way, to guard the way to the tree of life. (Genesis 3:22-24)

Adam and Eve After the Expulsion

By Julius Schnorr von Carolsfeld (Die Bibel in Bildern 1852-1860)

¹ Now Adam knew Eve his wife, and she conceived and bore Cain, and said, "I have acquired a man from the Lord." ² Then she bore again, this time his brother Abel. Now Abel was a keeper of sheep, but Cain was a tiller of the ground. (Genesis 4:1-2)

Cain and Abel's Offering

By Julius Schnorr von Carolsfeld (Die Bibel in Bildern 1852-1860)

3 And in the process of time it came to pass that Cain brought an offering of the fruit of the ground to the Lord. 4 Abel also brought of the firstborn of his flock and of their fat. And the Lord respected Abel and his offering, 5 but He did not respect Cain and his offering. And Cain was very angry, and his countenance fell. 6 So the Lord said to Cain, "Why are you angry? And why has your countenance fallen? 7 If you do well, will you not be accepted? And if you do not do well, sin lies at the door. And its desire is for you, but you should rule over it." (Genesis 4:3-7)

Cain Kills His Brother Abel

By Julius Schnorr von Carolsfeld (Die Bibel in Bildern 1852-1860)

[8] Now Cain talked with Abel his brother; and it came to pass, when they were in the field, that Cain rose up against Abel his brother and killed him. [9] Then the Lord said to Cain, Where is Abel your brother?" He said, "I do not know. Am I my brother's keeper?" [10] And He said, "What have you done? The voice of your brother's blood cries out to Me from the ground. [11] So now you are cursed from the earth, which has opened its mouth to receive your brother's blood from your hand. [12] When you till the ground, it shall no longer yield its strength to you. A fugitive and a vagabond you shall be on the earth."
(Genesis 4:8-12)

Adam and Eve:

Adam and Eve were told by God that they were free to eat from any tree in the garden except the tree of the knowledge of good and evil. But the man and the woman were seduced by the serpent into eating the forbidden fruit, and they were expelled from the garden to prevent them from eating of the tree of life, and thus living forever. The couple had three sons, Cain, Abel, and Seth.

Descendants of Cain and Seth:

[17] Cain had intercourse with his wife, and she conceived and bore Enoch. Cain also became the founder of a city, which he named after his son Enoch. [18] To Enoch was born Irad, and Irad became the father of Mehujael; Mehujael became the father of Methusael, and Methusael became the father of Lamech. [19] Lamech took two wives; the name of the first was Adah, and the name of the second Zillah. [20] Adah gave birth to Jabal, who became the ancestor of those who dwell in tents and keep livestock. [21] His brother's name was Jubal, who became the ancestor of all who play the lyre and the reed pipe. [22] Zillah, on her part, gave birth to Tubalcain, the ancestor of all who forge instruments of bronze and iron. The sister of Tubalcain was Naamah. [23] Lamech said to his wives: "Adah and Zillah, hear my voice; wives of Lamech, listen to my utterance: I have killed a man for wounding me, a young man for bruising me. [24] If Cain is avenged seven times, then Lamech seventy-seven times." [25] Adam again had intercourse with his wife, and she gave birth to a son whom she called Seth. "God has granted me another offspring in place of Abel," she said, "because Cain killed him." [26] To Seth, in turn, a son was born, and he named him Enosh. At that time people began to invoke the Lord by name. (Genesis 4:17-26)

The Prophecy of the Flood

By Julius Schnorr von Carolsfeld (Die Bibel in Bildern 1852-1860)

⁹ This is the genealogy of Noah. Noah was a just man, perfect in his generations. Noah walked with God. ¹⁰ And Noah begot three sons: Shem, Ham, and Japheth. ¹¹ The earth also was corrupt before God, and the earth was filled with violence. ¹² So God looked upon the earth, and indeed it was corrupt; for all flesh had corrupted their way on the earth. ¹³ And God said to Noah, "The end of all flesh has come before Me, for the earth is filled with violence through them; and behold, I will destroy them with the earth. (Genesis 6:9-13)

The Flood

By Julius Schnorr von Carolsfeld (Die Bibel in Bildern 1852-1860)

[17] Now the flood was on the earth forty days. The waters increased and lifted up the ark, and it rose high above the earth. [18] The waters prevailed and greatly increased on the earth, and the ark moved about on the surface of the waters. [19] And the waters prevailed exceedingly on the earth, and all the high hills under the whole heaven were covered. [20] The waters prevailed fifteen cubits upward, and the mountains were covered. [21] And all flesh died that moved on the earth: birds and cattle and beasts and every creeping thing that creeps on the earth, and every man. [22] All in whose nostrils was the breath of the spirit of life, all that was on the dry land, died. (Genesis 7:17-22)

The Ark Rests Upon Ararat

By Julius Schnorr von Carolsfeld (Die Bibel in Bildern 1852-1860)

[1] Then God remembered Noah, and every living thing, and all the animals that were with him in the ark. And God made a wind to pass over the earth, and the waters subsided. [2] The fountains of the deep and the windows of heaven were also stopped, and the rain from heaven was restrained. [3] And the waters receded continually from the earth. At the end of the hundred and fifty days the waters decreased. [4] Then the ark rested in the seventh month, the seventeenth day of the month, on the mountains of Ararat. [5] And the waters decreased continually until the tenth month. In the tenth month, on the first day of the month, the tops of the mountains were seen. (Genesis 8:1-5)

Covenant Theology:

Covenant Theology is a common structure for Biblical study in Protestant groups, specifically in Presbyterian and Reformed churches. A similar form is also found in Methodist and Reformed Baptist churches. Covenant theology is a bit different model in understanding the structure of the Bible. It uses the theological covenant concept as an organizing principle. The standard form of covenant theology looks at the history of the relationship between God and his people using three conceptual theological frameworks of redemption, of works, and of grace. Covenant theologians organize history and theology around covenants, or arrangements between God and His people.

The Covenant of Redemption occurred before creation. It refers to the covenant within the Trinity that established the plan of salvation for all believers. The agreement was within the Godhead that the Father would appoint the Son to give up his life for mankind and the Son's agreement to do so. Aside from the promise of salvation, the promise that the Holy Spirit would be given to the Church and that the Son would be exalted.

From the Book of Titus, a missionary of Paul, in the New Testament:

[1] Paul, a servant of God and an apostle of Jesus Christ to further the faith of God's elect and their knowledge of the truth that leads to godliness— [2] in the hope of eternal life, which God, who does not lie, promised before the beginning of time, [3] and which now at his appointed season he has brought to light through the preaching entrusted to me by the command of God our Savior, (Titus 1:1-3)

The Covenant of Works is the pre-Fall agreement between Adam and God. Adam was promised blessing and life if he was obedient to the terms of the covenant and cursing and death should he disobey, which he did.

[15] The Lord God took the man and put him in the Garden of Eden to work it and take care of it. [16] And the Lord God commanded the man, "You are free to eat from any tree in the garden; [17] but you must not eat from the tree of the knowledge of good and evil, for when you eat from it you will certainly die." (Genesis 2:15-17)

The Covenant of Grace promised eternal blessing for belief in Jesus Christ and obedience to God. For Christians, it is considered a basic for all covenants made between God and man, Noah, Abraham, David, with Israel as a people, and with Christians in the New Covenant. This promised eternal blessing for belief in Christ and obedience to God's word.

From the Book of Jeremiah, long before Jesus Christ:

[31] "The days are coming," declares the Lord, "when I will make a new covenant with the people of Israel and with the people of Judah. [32] It will not be like the covenant I made with their ancestors when I took them by the hand to lead them out of Egypt, because they broke my covenant, though I was a husband to them," declares the Lord. [33] "This is the covenant I will make with the people of Israel after that time," declares the Lord. "I will put my law in their minds and write it on their hearts. I will be their God, and they will be my people. (Jeremiah 31:31-33)

The New Covenant of Grace was also throughout the New Testament:

[19] Then he took the bread, said the blessing, broke it, and gave it to them, saying, "This is my body, which will be given for you; do this in memory of me." [20] And likewise the cup after they had eaten, saying, "This cup is the new covenant in my blood, which will be shed for you. (Luke 22:19-20)

²² No, you have approached Mount Zion and the city of the living God, the heavenly Jerusalem, and countless angels in festal gathering, ²³ and the assembly of the firstborn enrolled in heaven, and God the judge of all, and the spirits of the just made perfect, ²⁴ and Jesus, the mediator of a new covenant, and the sprinkled blood that speaks more eloquently than that of Abel. (Hebrews 12:22-24)

⁵ Not that of ourselves we are qualified to take credit for anything as coming from us; rather, our qualification comes from God, ⁶ who has indeed qualified us as ministers of a new covenant, not of letter but of spirit; for the letter brings death, but the Spirit gives life. (2 Corinthians 3:5-6)

***

Dispensational Theology:

Another common method used for Biblical analysis is called Dispensational theology, a practice followed by early Christian fundamentalists in defense against the religious liberalism and modernism. Dispensational theology views Biblical history as being divided by God into dispensations, which are defined periods or epochs to which God has distinct purposes. Each age is administered differently, and humanity is held responsible as a steward during that time. This structure maintains focus on history portraying the glory of God and God at its core, rather than a focus on man and humanity's need for redemption and salvation, such as with the covenant theology view. In dispensational thought each epoch is cyclical and divinely inspired. Each has four characteristics: 1) God reveals himself and his truth to man; 2) man is held responsible to conform to that truth; 3) humanity rebels and fails God's test morally and spiritually; 4) God judges humanity and introduces a new period of repentance, deliverance and renewal under new leadership. Each period represents a different method or test in which God deals with humanity and each one ends in a judgment of man. The number of dispensations noted in Biblical study vary between three to eight, although seven dispensations are commonly noted.

***

1) **The Dispensation of Innocence** (Genesis) The Creation to the Expulsion. Adam and Eve defied God and ate from the Tree of the Knowledge of Good and Evil. Final judgement is expulsion from Eden. Adamic covenant is broken.

2) **The Dispensation of Conscience** (Genesis) The Fall to the Great Flood. Cain killed Abel defying God's law. Final judge is the deluge. Noahic covenant with God is broken.

3) **The Dispensation of Government** (Genesis) From the Deluge to the Tower of Babel. People disobeyed God's law by building a tower tall enough to reach God and heaven. People failed to live by own conscious and establish just government. Final judgement is the language dispersion and confusion.

4) **Dispensation of Promise** (Genesis) From Abraham to Moses. People failed to remain faithful to Yahweh alone. Abrahamic Covenant/Law with God is broken. Final judgment is slavery in Egypt and forty years in the desert.

5) **Dispensation of Law** (Exodus) From Moses to Jesus Christ. The people were unfaithful to God by having Jesus crucified. Mosaic Covenant/Law with God is broken. Judgement ends with the scattering of Israel in 70AD.

6) **The Dispensation of Grace or the Church** (future) From Crucifixion-Pentecost until the Rapture-Great Tribulation. Final judgment is the great tribulation, a future society. denoting afflictions, disease, famine, and war.

7) **The Dispensation of Kingdom** (future) The Abrahamic promise continues with a millennial reign of Jesus Christ on earth centered in Jerusalem, with a time characterized by peace, justice, abundance, healing, righteousness, and unity. It ends with God's judgment with the final battle on the last day.

***

Covenantal Theology:

The Catholic Church however, uses a system called Covenantal theology for interpreting Scripture. All three systems are different in focus, but all worthy of mentioning in order to stress the importance of God's covenants with his chosen people. Covenantal theology is a distinct traditional approach to biblical analysis that the Catholic Church has used for centuries. It has roots in what is called Patristics, the study of the early Christian Church Fathers. These early Christian scholars used exegesis and hermeneutics to interpret Scripture. *Exegesis* in Greek means to lead out, it offers a critical explanation of a religious writing. It includes a range of disciplines such as textual criticism which looks at the history and origins of the text. It may also include the study of the historical and cultural backgrounds of the author, text, and original audience. Other analyses include classification of the type of literary genres and grammatical and syntactical features in the text itself.

Hermeneutics is the methodology of interpretation of biblical texts and philosophical writings. Modern hermeneutics includes both verbal and non-verbal communication as well as semiotics, presuppositions, and pre-understandings. The terms hermeneutics and exegesis are sometimes used interchangeably, although hermeneutics covers a wider field which includes written, verbal, and non-verbal communication. Exegesis focuses primarily upon the word and grammar of texts. A revival of medieval exegesis during the mid-20th century coincided with publication of *Dei verbum*, at the Second Vatican Council's *Dogmatic Constitution on Divine Revelation*, promoted by Pope Paul VI in 1965 which strongly revived the biblical analysis form. The later Catechism of the Catholic Church (1994, 1997) also reinforced this teaching specifying the necessity of the spiritual interpretation of Scripture to be experienced through the *four senses, the literal sense, and three* spiritual senses (allegorical, moral, anagogical). This approach emphasizes the four senses of Scripture within a framework of salvation history with the Biblical covenants and studied in combination with modern techniques.

The Covenant of the Rainbow

By Julius Schnorr von Carolsfeld (Die Bibel in Bildern 1852-1860)

[8] Then God spoke to Noah and to his sons with him, saying: [9] "And as for Me, behold, I establish My covenant with you and with your descendants after you, [10] and with every living creature that is with you: the birds, the cattle, and every beast of the earth with you, of all that go out of the ark, every beast of the earth. [11] Thus I establish My covenant with you: Never again shall all flesh be cut off by the waters of the flood; never again shall there be a flood to destroy the earth." (Genesis 9:8-11)

The Tower of Babel

By Julius Schnorr von Carolsfeld (Die Bibel in Bildern 1852-1860)

¹ Now the whole earth had one language and one speech. ² And it came to pass, as they journeyed from the east, that they found a plain in the land of Shinar, and they dwelt there. ³ Then they said to one another, "Come, let us make bricks and bake them thoroughly." They had brick for stone, and they had asphalt for mortar. ⁴ And they said, "Come, let us build ourselves a city, and a tower whose top is in the heavens; let us make a name for ourselves, lest we be scattered abroad over the face of the earth". (Genesis 11:1-4)

III. Patriarchal History (11:27-50:26)

The Patriarchal History covers the history of the patriarchs and can be considered myth, legend, or historical documentation depending on personal interpretation. At minimum the patriarchs are Abraham, Isaac, and Jacob, although broadly it can include up to twenty male ancestors between Adam and Abraham. The antediluvian period, between the fall of man and the flood, include ten generations:

0 - Adam is created (generation 1)

130 - Adam and Eve third son, Seth (generation 2)

235 - Enosh is born (generation 3)

325 - Kenan is born (generation 4)

395 - Mahalaleel is born (generation 5)

460 - Jared is born (generation 6)

622 - Enoch is born (generation 7)

687 - Methuselah is born (generation 8)

874 - Lamech is born (generation 9)

1056 - Noah is born (generation 10)

1556 – Noah's three sons: Shem, Ham, Japheth (generation 11)

1658 - Arpachshad is born (generation 12)

1693 - Shelah is born (generation 13)

1723 - Eber is born (generation 14)

1757 - Peleg is born (generation 15)

1787 - Reu is born (generation 16)

1819 - Serug is born (generation 17)

1849 - Nahor is born (generation 18)

1878 - Terah is born (generation 19)

1948 - Abraham is born (generation 20)

Abram/Abraham:

Abraham is the common patriarchal figure of the three monotheistic religions. In Judaism, he is the ancestor of Adam, and father of the covenant between the Jewish people and God; in Christianity, he is the Jewish ancestor of Jesus whose line travels back to Adam; and in Islam he is the birth father of Ishmael, an ancestor of Muhammad whose line also dates back to Adam. The story of Abraham is not definitively related to any specific historical period. Biblical scholarly consensus is that it is a later literary construct composed in the 6th century BC during the Persian era. The story in Genesis revolves around the theme of land ownership, so it is understandable that Jewish land disputes resulting from the Babylonian split of the Hebrew people, may have influenced the narrative. According to Jewish tradition, Abraham was born in the city of Ur of the Chaldees in Babylonia 1948 years after the creation, which would be about 1800BC. He was the son of Terach (Terah) who was ironically, an idol merchant. Besides Abraham, Terach also fathered Nahor and Haran, and a daughter Sarai with a second wife.

God calls Abraham to leave the house of his father and travel to Canaan. He marries his half-sister Sarai, who is barren. Abraham has a son, Ismael, with Sarai's slave girl, Hagar. Sarai later conceives and gives birth to a son, Isaac, through a covenant with God, who then changes her name to Sarah. Although promises are made to Ishmael about becoming the leader of a great nation, it is Isaac, who inherits God's promise made to his father. Abraham purchases a tomb (the Cave of the Patriarchs) at Hebron to be Sarah's grave, which established him rights to the land. After Sarah dies, he marries Keturah, a concubine, and has six more sons. However, at his death, it is Isaac who receives all the land that God promised to his father, while the other sons receive only gifts.

[5] Abraham gave everything that he owned to his son Isaac. [6] To the sons of his concubines, however, he gave gifts while he was still living, as he sent them away eastward, to the land of Kedem, away from son Isaac. (Genesis 25:5-6)

Abraham: Covenant of Circumcision:

¹ When Abram was ninety-nine years old, the Lord appeared to Abram and said: I am God the Almighty. Walk in my presence and be blameless. ² Between you and me I will establish my covenant, and I will multiply you exceedingly. ³ Abram fell face down and God said to him: ⁴ For my part, here is my covenant with you: you are to become the father of a multitude of nations. ⁵ No longer will you be called Abram; your name will be Abraham, for I am making you the father of a multitude of nations. ⁶ I will make you exceedingly fertile; I will make nations of you; kings will stem from you. ⁷ I will maintain my covenant between me and you and your descendants after you throughout the ages as an everlasting covenant, to be your God and the God of your descendants after you. ⁸ I will give to you and to your descendants after you the land in which you are now residing as aliens, the whole land of Canaan, as a permanent possession; and I will be their God. ⁹ God said to Abraham: For your part, you and your descendants after you must keep my covenant throughout the ages. ¹⁰ This is the covenant between me and you and your descendants after you that you must keep: every male among you shall be circumcised. ¹¹ Circumcise the flesh of your foreskin. That will be the sign of the covenant between me and you. ¹² Throughout the ages, every male among you, when he is eight days old, shall be circumcised, including house born slaves and those acquired with money from any foreigner who is not of your descendants. ¹³ Yes, both the house born slaves and those acquired with money must be circumcised. Thus, my covenant will be in your flesh as an everlasting covenant. ¹⁴ If a male is uncircumcised, that is, if the flesh of his foreskin has not been cut away, such a one will be cut off from his people; he has broken my covenant. (Genesis 17:1-14)

God's Promise to Abram

By Julius Schnorr von Carolsfeld (Die Bibel in Bildern 1852-1860)

¹ Now the Lord had said to Abram: "Get out of your country, From your family and from your father's house, To a land that I will show you. ² I will make you a great nation; I will bless you and make your name great; And you shall be a blessing. ³ I will bless those who bless you, And I will curse him who curses you; And in you all the families of the earth shall be blessed." (Genesis 12:1-3)

Abram Receives the First Promise

By Julius Schnorr von Carolsfeld (Die Bibel in Bildern 1852-1860)

[7] Then the Lord appeared to Abram and said, "To your descendants I will give this land." And there he built an altar to the Lord, who had appeared to him. [8] And he moved from there to the mountain east of Bethel, and he pitched his tent with Bethel on the west and Ai on the east; there he built an altar to the Lord and called on the name of the Lord. [9] So Abram journeyed, going on still toward the South. (Genesis 12:7-9)

Ishmael:

According to Jews, Christians, and Muslims, Ishmael was Abraham's first son. He was born to Sarah's handmaiden Hagar. The Book of Genesis and Islamic tradition name Ishmael as the ancestor of the Ishmaelites and patriarch of Qaydar, an ancient Arab tribal confederation that controlled the region between the Persian Gulf and Sinai Peninsula during the 6th century BC. The term Arab, similar to the term Hebrew, describes a people's language, rather than a culture or ethnic group. Muslim tradition holds that Ishmael and his mother Hagar are buried next to the Kaaba in the Al-Haram Mosque in Mecca. After Sarah became jealous of Hagar and her son Ishmael, thinking that the boy would inherit the land rather than her own son, Isaac, she forced Abraham to exile the two from the tribe.

[3] Thus, after Abram had lived ten years in the land of Canaan, his wife Sarai took her maid, Hagar the Egyptian, and gave her to her husband Abram to be his wife. (Genesis 16:3)

[9] Sarah noticed the son whom Hagar the Egyptian had borne to Abraham playing with her son Isaac; [10] so she demanded of Abraham: "Drive out that slave and her son! No son of that slave is going to share the inheritance with my son Isaac!" [11] Abraham was greatly distressed because it concerned a son of his. [12] But God said to Abraham: Do not be distressed about the boy or about your slave woman. Obey Sarah, no matter what she asks of you; for it is through Isaac that descendants will bear your name. [13] As for the son of the slave woman, I will make a nation of him also, since he too is your offspring. (Genesis 21:9-13)

***

8 Then he breathed his last, dying at a ripe old age, grown old after a full life; and he was gathered to his people. 9 His sons Isaac and Ishmael buried him in the cave of Machpelah, in the field of Ephron, son of Zohar the Hittite, which faces Mamre, 10 the field that Abraham had bought from the Hittites; there he was buried next to his wife Sarah. (Genesis 25:8-10)

After roaming the wilderness, Ishmael and his mother Hagar settled in the Desert of Paran. He married an Egyptian woman who he had twelve sons with: Nebaioth, Kedar, Adbeel, Mibsam, Mishma, Dumah, Massa, Hadad, Tema, Jetur, Naphish, and Kedemah. Tradition holds that Kedar was the father of the Qedarites and ancestor of the Islamic prophet, Muhammad. Ishmael also had a daughter, Mahalath (Basemath), the third wife of Esau. Ishmael also appeared with Isaac at the burial of Abraham.

13 These are the names of Ishmael's sons, listed in the order of their birth: Ishmael's firstborn Nebaioth, Kedar, Adbeel, Mibsam, 14 Mishma, Dumah, Massa, 15 Hadad, Tema, Jetur, Naphish, and Kedemah. 16 These are the sons of Ishmael, their names by their villages and encampments; twelve chieftains of as many tribal groups. 17 The span of Ishmael's life was one hundred and thirty-seven years. After he had breathed his last and died, he was gathered to his people. 18 The Ishmaelites ranged from Havilah, by Shur, which is on the border of Egypt, all the way to Asshur; and they pitched camp alongside their various kindred. (Genesis 25:13-18)

Abraham Receives God's Promise of a Son

By Julius Schnorr von Carolsfeld (Die Bibel in Bildern 1852-1860)

[9] *Then God said: "No, Sarah your wife shall bear you a son, and you shall call his name Isaac; I will establish My covenant with him for an everlasting covenant, and with his descendants after him.* [20] *And as for Ishmael, I have heard you. Behold, I have blessed him, and will make him fruitful, and will multiply him exceedingly. He shall beget twelve princes, and I will make him a great nation.* [21] *But My covenant I will establish with Isaac, whom Sarah shall bear to you at this set time next year."* [22] *Then He finished talking with him, and God went up from Abraham. (Genesis 17:9-22)*

The Sacrifice of Isaac

By Julius Schnorr von Carolsfeld (Die Bibel in Bildern 1852-1860)

[15] Then the Angel of the Lord called to Abraham a second time out of heaven, [16] and said: "By Myself I have sworn, says the Lord, because you have done this thing, and have not withheld your son, your only son— [17] blessing I will bless you, and multiplying I will multiply your descendants as the stars of the heaven and as the sand which is on the seashore; and your descendants shall possess the gate of their enemies. [18] In your seed all the nations of the earth shall be blessed, because you have obeyed My voice." [19] So Abraham returned to his young men, and they rose and went together to Beersheba; and Abraham dwelt at Beersheba. (Genesis 22:15-19)

Isaac:

His name means *he will laugh*, which reflects Sarah laughing in disbelief when told that she would have a child. Isaac is the only patriarch whose name was not changed and the only one who did not leave Canaan. He was also the only patriarch who had only one wife. His father, Abraham, did not want Isaac to wed a Canaanite woman so he sent his servant to his home town of Nahor to find a wife for his son. Rebekah, daughter of Bethuel, was brought back for Isaac. He was thirty-six when his mother died, and he took Rebekah as his wife. For many years Isaac and Rebekah were childless, but eventually Rebekah gave birth to twin boys, Jacob and Esau.

¹ Abraham was old, having seen many days, and the Lord had blessed him in every way. ² Abraham said to the senior servant of his household, who had charge of all his possessions: "Put your hand under my thigh, ³ and I will make you swear by the Lord, the God of heaven and the God of earth, that you will not take a wife for my son from the daughters of the Canaanites among whom I live, ⁴ but that you will go to my own land and to my relatives to get a wife for my son Isaac." (Genesis 24:1-4)

¹⁹ These are the descendants of Isaac, son of Abraham; Abraham begot Isaac. ²⁰ Isaac was forty years old when he married Rebekah, the daughter of Bethuel the Aramean of Paddan-aram and the sister of Laban the Aramean. ²¹ Isaac entreated the LORD on behalf of his wife, since she was sterile. The LORD heard his entreaty, and his wife Rebekah became pregnant. ²² But the children jostled each other in the womb so much that she exclaimed, "If it is like this, why go on living!" She went to consult the Lord, ²³ and the Lord answered her: Two nations are in your womb, two peoples are separating while still within you; but one will be stronger than the other, and the older will serve the younger. (Genesis 25:19-23)

Rebekah Gives Abraham's Servant Water

By Julius Schnorr von Carolsfeld (Die Bibel in Bildern 1852-1860)

[15] And it happened, before he had finished speaking, that behold, Rebekah, who was born to Bethuel, son of Milcah, the wife of Nahor, Abraham's brother, came out with her pitcher on her shoulder. [16] Now the young woman was very beautiful to behold, a virgin; no man had known her. And she went down to the well, filled her pitcher, and came up. [17] And the servant ran to meet her and said, "Please let me drink a little water from your pitcher." (Genesis 24:15-17)

Isaac Is Deceived by Jacob

By Julius Schnorr von Carolsfeld (Die Bibel in Bildern 1852-1860)

[13] But his mother said to him, "Let your curse be on me, my son; only obey my voice, and go, get them for me." [14] And he went and got them and brought them to his mother, and his mother made [c]savory food, such as his father loved. [15] Then Rebekah took the choice clothes of her elder son Esau, which were with her in the house, and put them on Jacob her younger son. [16] And she put the skins of the kids of the goats on his hands and on the smooth part of his neck. [17] Then she gave the savory food and the bread, which she had prepared, into the hand of her son Jacob. (Genesis 27:13-17)

Jacob's Dream

By Julius Schnorr von Carolsfeld (Die Bibel in Bildern 1852-1860)

[10] *Jacob departed from Beersheba and proceeded toward Haran.* [11] *When he came upon a certain place, he stopped there for the night, since the sun had already set. Taking one of the stones at the place, he put it under his head and lay down in that place.* [12] *Then he had a dream: a stairway rested on the ground, with its top reaching to the heavens; and God's angels were going up and down on it.* [13] *And there was the Lord standing beside him and saying: I am the Lord, the God of Abraham your father and the God of Isaac; the land on which you are lying I will give to you and your descendants.* [14] *Your descendants will be like the dust of the earth, and through them you will spread to the west and the east, to the north and the south. In you and your descendants all the families of the earth will find blessing. (Genesis 28:10-14)*

Jacob and Rachel at the Well

By Julius Schnorr von Carolsfeld (Die Bibel in Bildern 1852-1860)

⁹ Now while he was still speaking with them, Rachel came with her father's sheep, for she was a shepherdess. ¹⁰ And it came to pass, when Jacob saw Rachel the daughter of Laban his mother's brother, and the sheep of Laban his mother's brother, that Jacob went near and rolled the stone from the well's mouth and watered the flock of Laban his mother's brother. ¹¹ Then Jacob kissed Rachel and lifted up his voice and wept. ¹² And Jacob told Rachel that he was her father's relative and that he was Rebekah's son. So she ran and told her father. (Genesis 29:9-12)

Esau and Jacob:

Isaac was sixty years old when the twin boys were born. Rebekah's two sons could not have been any more different. Esau was a rugged hunter, rough looking, and very hairy. He had at least three wives, two of which were Canaanite women, which went against Isaac's wishes. Esau was born first therefore should have inherited Isaac's blessing and land. However, Jacob was very close to his mother and to God. With some coaxing from Rebekah, Jacob deceives his father into giving him the blessing on his deathbed, rather than Esau. Esau becomes infuriated and separates from his brother, only to become father and leader of the Edomites, the line that eventually gives rise to the tribe of Mohammed in the Muslim faith. Esau had five sons.

[1] These are the descendants of Esau (that is, Edom). [2] Esau took his wives from among the Canaanite women: Adah, daughter of Elon the Hittite; Oholibamah, the daughter of Anah the son of Zibeon the Hivite; [3] and Basemath, daughter of Ishmael and sister of Nebaioth. [4] Adah bore Eliphaz to Esau; Basemath bore Reuel; [5] and Oholibamah bore Jeush, Jalam and Korah. These are the sons of Esau who were born to him in the land of Canaan. [6] Esau took his wives, his sons, his daughters, and all the members of his household, as well as his livestock, all his cattle, and all the property he had acquired in the land of Canaan, and went to the land of Seir, away from his brother Jacob. [7] Their possessions had become too great for them to dwell together, and the land in which they were residing could not support them because of their livestock. [8] So Esau settled in the highlands of Seir. (Esau is Edom.) (Genesis 36:1-8)

Jacob had twelve sons and at least one daughter. His two wives, Leah and Rachael, were sisters, both daughters of Laban, who was sister to Jacob's mother, Rebekah. Jacob also had children with two of his wives' handmaidens, Bilhah and Zilpah. The twelve sons eventually become the forefathers of the Twelve Tribes of Israel.

His son Joseph was favored by his father, Jacob. And in a streak of jealousy the boy is sold into slavery by his brothers and taken to Egypt. Years later, a severe drought in Canaan, led the brothers to Egypt in search of food. Joseph, who had worked his way into the pharaohs palace as viceroy, reunites with the brothers who betrayed him. Jacob had been lied to and thought Joseph to be dead. But Joseph forgave his brothers, gave them food, and welcomed them into Egypt to stay. Jacob lasted seventeen years there before dying. Joseph carried his father's remains back to Canaan, where he was buried in the same Cave of Machpelah with Abraham, Sarah, Isaac, Rebecca, and Jacob's first wife, Leah. Many of the Israelite people ended up staying in Egypt and the numbers grew. But they became marginalized, persecuted, and eventually enslaved by the Egyptians. This captivity lasted four hundred years until Moses led them back to the Promised Land of Canaan.

[20] So Joseph acquired all the land of Egypt for Pharaoh. Each of the Egyptians sold his field, since the famine weighed heavily upon them. Thus the land passed over to Pharaoh, [21] and the people were reduced to slavery, from one end of Egypt's territory to the other. [22] Only the priests' lands Joseph did not acquire. Since the priests had a fixed allowance from Pharaoh and lived off the allowance Pharaoh had granted them, they did not have to sell their land. [23] Joseph told the people: "Now that I have acquired you and your land for Pharaoh, here is your seed for sowing the land. [24] But when the harvest is in, you must give a fifth of it to Pharaoh, while you keep four-fifths as seed for your fields and as food for yourselves and your households and as food for your children." [25] "You have saved our lives!" they answered. "We have found favor with my lord; now we will be Pharaoh's slaves." [26] Thus Joseph made it a statute for the land of Egypt, which is still in force, that a fifth of its produce should go to Pharaoh. Only the land of the priests did not pass over to Pharaoh. (Genesis 47:20-26)

Jacob Wrestles with the Angel

By Julius Schnorr von Carolsfeld (Die Bibel in Bildern 1852-1860)

[23] *That night, however, Jacob arose, took his two wives, with the two maidservants and his eleven children, and crossed the ford of the Jabbok. [24] After he got them and brought them across the wadi and brought over what belonged to him, [25] Jacob was left there alone. Then a man wrestled with him until the break of dawn. [26] When the man saw that he could not prevail over him, he struck Jacob's hip at its socket, so that Jacob's socket was dislocated as he wrestled with him. [27] The man then said, "Let me go, for it is daybreak." But Jacob said, "I will not let you go until you bless me." [28] "What is your name?" the man asked. He answered, "Jacob." [29] Then the man said, "You shall no longer be named Jacob, but Israel, because you have contended with divine and human beings and have prevailed." (Genesis 32:23-29)*

Jacob's Reconciliation with Esau

By Julius Schnorr von Carolsfeld (Die Bibel in Bildern 1852-1860)

⁴ Jacob sent messengers ahead to his brother Esau in the land of Seir, the country of Edom, ⁵ ordering them: "Thus you shall say to my lord Esau: 'Thus says your servant Jacob: I have been residing with Laban and have been delayed until now. ⁶ I own oxen, donkeys and sheep, as well as male and female servants. I have sent my lord this message in the hope of gaining your favor.'" ⁷ When the messengers returned to Jacob, they said, "We found your brother Esau. He is now coming to meet you, and four hundred men with him." (Genesis 32:4-7)

Joseph is Sold into Egypt

By Julius Schnorr von Carolsfeld (Die Bibel in Bildern 1852-1860)

[28] Midianite traders passed by, and they pulled Joseph up out of the cistern. They sold Joseph for twenty pieces of silver to the Ishmaelites, who took him to Egypt. [29] When Reuben went back to the cistern and saw that Joseph was not in it, he tore his garments, [30] and returning to his brothers, he exclaimed: "The boy is gone! And I—where can I turn?" [31] They took Joseph's tunic, and after slaughtering a goat, dipped the tunic in its blood. [32] Then they sent someone to bring the long-ornamented tunic to their father, with the message: "We found this. See whether it is your son's tunic or not." [33] He recognized it and exclaimed: "My son's tunic! A wild beast has devoured him! Joseph has been torn to pieces!" (Genesis 37:28-33)

Joseph Interprets Pharaoh's Dream

By Julius Schnorr von Carolsfeld (Die Bibel in Bildern 1852-1860)

[17] Then Pharaoh said to Joseph: "In my dream, I was standing on the bank of the Nile, [18] when up from the Nile came seven cows, fat and well-formed; they grazed in the reed grass. [19] Behind them came seven other cows, scrawny, most ill-formed and gaunt. Never have I seen such bad specimens as these in all the land of Egypt! [20] The gaunt, bad cows devoured the first seven fat cows. [21] But when they had consumed them, no one could tell that they had done so, because they looked as bad as before. Then I woke up. [22] In another dream I saw seven ears of grain, full and healthy, growing on a single stalk. [23] Behind them sprouted seven ears of grain, shriveled and thin and scorched by the east wind; [24] and the seven thin ears swallowed up the seven healthy ears. I have spoken to the magicians, but there is no one to explain it to me."
(Genesis 41:17-24)

Joseph is Ruler Over All Egypt

By Julius Schnorr von Carolsfeld (Die Bibel in Bildern 1852-1860)

[37] This advice pleased Pharaoh and all his servants. [38] "Could we find another like him," Pharaoh asked his servants, "a man so endowed with the spirit of God?" [39] So Pharaoh said to Joseph: "Since God has made all this known to you, there is no one as discerning and wise as you are. [40] You shall oversee my household, and all my people will obey your command. Only in respect to the throne will I outrank you." [41] Then Pharaoh said to Joseph, "Look, I put you in charge of the whole land of Egypt." [42] With that, Pharaoh took off his signet ring and put it on Joseph's finger. He dressed him in robes of fine linen and put a gold chain around his neck. [43] He then had him ride in his second chariot, and they shouted "Abrek!" before him. (Genesis 41:37-43)

Joseph Reveals Himself to His Brothers

By Julius Schnorr von Carolsfeld (Die Bibel in Bildern 1852-1860)

4 "Come closer to me," Joseph told his brothers. When they had done so, he said: "I am your brother Joseph, whom you sold into Egypt. 5 But now do not be distressed, and do not be angry with yourselves for having sold me here. It was really for the sake of saving lives that God sent me here ahead of you. 6 The famine has been in the land for two years now, and for five more years cultivation will yield no harvest. 7 God, therefore, sent me on ahead of you to ensure for you a remnant on earth and to save your lives in an extraordinary deliverance. 8 So it was not really you but God who had me come here; and he has made me a father to Pharaoh, lord of all his household, and ruler over the whole land of Egypt. (Genesis 45:4-8)

The Twelve Tribes of Israel:

After the death of Moses, under the leadership of Joshua, the Twelve Tribes of Israel take possession of the Promised Land of Canaan. The twelve tribes are named after sons or grandsons of Jacob, whose name was changed to Israel after he wrestled with the Angel of the Lord. The Hebrew people then became known as the Israelites to be led by Jacob. Jacob's first wife, Leah, bore him six sons: Reuben, Simeon, Levi, Judah, Issachar, and Zebulun. Each was the father of a tribe. Among Levi's descendants were Moses and Aaron. The priests and other temple positions were dispersed among the other tribes and received no land of their own.

Two other tribes, Gad and Asher, were named after sons born to Jacob and Zilpah, Leah's maidservant. Two additional tribes, Dan and Naphtali, were named after sons of Jacob born of Bilhah, the maidservant of Rachel, Jacob's second wife. Rachel bore Jacob two sons, Joseph and Benjamin. The tribe of Benjamin provided Israel with its first king, Saul, and was later assimilated into the tribe of Judah. While no tribe bore the name of Joseph, two tribes were named after Joseph's sons, Manasseh and Ephraim. Ten tribes settled in northern Palestine but were captured by the Assyrians, known as the Ten Lost Tribes of Israel. The Twelve Tribes of Israel include ten of the sons of Jacob (excluding Levi and Joseph) and the two sons of Joseph.

To put it in historical context, Joseph lived about 1850 BC, Moses about 1450 BC, and Solomon about 950 BC. On the succession of Solomon's son, Rehoboam, around 930 BC, the Kingdom of Israel that was united under Saul, David, and Solomon, then split into two kingdoms. The Kingdom of Israel (Samaria) in the north and the Kingdom of Judah (Jerusalem) in the south, which continued for about two centuries. The northern kingdom was greatly influenced by Babylonian culture and emerged as a power during the tenth century BC. The southern kingdom emerged about a century later. In 586 BC the Babylonians pushed the southern Jews to the point of revolt which led to the exile of some of the northern Jews to Babylon. In 539 BC Cyrus the Great freed them from exile and led them back to Jerusalem.

Through the 4th to 2nd centuries BC. the Ptolemies of Egypt and Seleucids of Syria competed for power and intermarried for succession. Greek culture with Alexander's conquests infiltrated much of the area by about 340 BC and lasted until the Romans marched into the area during the first century BC.

- Terah (descendant of Shem), father of Abram, Nahor, and Haran
  - Abram and Hagar, parents of Ishmael (Ishmaelites)
  - Abram and Keturah, parents of Zimran, Jokshan, Medan, Midian, (Midianites), Ishbak, Shuah
  - Nahor and Milcah, parents of Uz, Buz, Kemuel, Kesed, Hazo, Pildash, Jidlaph, and Bethuel
  - Kemuel, father of Aram (Arameans)
  - Bethuel, father of Laban and Rebeccah
  - Laban, father of Leah and Rachel
    - Nahor and Reumah, parents of Tebah, Gaham, Tahash, Maacab
    - Haran, father of Lot
  - Lot and his older daughter, parents of Moab (Moabites)
  - Lot and his younger daughter, parents of Ben-ammi (Ammonites)
- Abraham and Sarah, parents of Isaac
- Isaac and Rebekah, parents of Jacob, Esau (Edomites)
  - Esau and Adah, parents of Eliphaz
  - Eliphaz and Timna, parents of Amalek (Amalekites)
  - Jacob and Leah, parents of Reuben, Simeon, Levi, Judah, Issachar, Zebulun, Dina
  - Jacob and Rachel, parents of Joseph, Benjamin
  - Jacob and Bilhah, parents of Dan, Naphtali
  - Jacob and Zilpah, parents of Gad, Asher
  - Joseph and Asenath, parents of Manasseh, Ephraim

Jacob Comes into Egypt

By Julius Schnorr von Carolsfeld (Die Bibel in Bildern 1852-1860)

[5] *So Jacob departed from Beersheba, and the sons of Israel put their father and their wives and children on the wagons that Pharaoh had sent to transport him.* [6] *They took with them their livestock and the possessions they had acquired in the land of Canaan. So, Jacob and all his descendants came to Egypt.* [7] *His sons and his grandsons, his daughters and his granddaughters —all his descendants—he took with him to Egypt. (Genesis 46:5-7)*

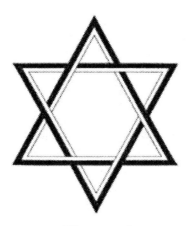

Chapter 3
The Book of Exodus

(Shemot / Names)
11 Parashot / 40 Chapters

Parashah	Hebrew	English	Chapter/Line
13	Shemot	Names	Exodus 1:1-6:1
14	Va'eira	Appeared	6:2-9:35
15	Bo	Go	10:1-13:16
16	Beshalach	When he sent out	13:17-17:16
17	Yitro	Jethro	18:1-20:23
18	Mishpatim	Laws	21:1-24:18
19	Terumah	Offering	25:1-27:19
20	Tetzaveh	You shall command	27:20-30:10
21	Ki Tisa	When you elevate	30:11-34:35
22	Vayakhel	And he assembled	35:1-38:20
23	Pekudei	Accountings	38:21-40:38

***

The word Exodus is a Greek word, *exodos*, meaning *going out* or *departure*. The title was retained by the Vulgate, the fourth-century Latin translation that became the Catholic Church's official version of the Bible during the 16th century. In Hebrew, *we'elleh shemoth*, means *these are the names of.* The text proceeds to list those who traveled out of Egypt with Moses and Jacob. The narrative in Exodus was not intended to stand alone, but to be a continuation of the story in Genesis of the people of Israel. Several statements in Exodus indicate that Moses wrote sections of the book. Some Gospel passages in the New Testament also suggests that Moses penned much of the book. Although some modern religious scholars may argue against Moses authorship of the Pentateuch as a whole, there are many references that strongly suggest that he was at the least, the author of the Book of Exodus.

The exact chronology is not really known concerning the time of the Exodus from Egypt, although the First Book of Kings in the Historical Books states:

[1] In the four hundred and eightieth year after the Israelites went forth from the land of Egypt, in the fourth year of Solomon's reign over Israel, in the month of Ziv (second month), he began to build the house of the Lord. (1 Kings 6:1)

Since that year was 966 BC, it has been traditionally held that the exodus occurred 1446 66BC. Egyptian chronology suggests that two of the 18th dynasty pharaohs, Thutmose III and his son Amunhotep II, ruled during the oppression and exodus. Although the name Rameses appear in other passages throughout the Book of Exodus, which would mean that it happened during the 19th-dynasty under the rule of pharaoh Seti I and his son Rameses II.

I. Prologue (ch1-2)

Jacob's Descendants in Egypt:

[1] These are the names of the sons of Israel who, accompanied by their households, entered into Egypt with Jacob: [2] Reuben, Simeon, Levi and Judah; [3] Issachar, Zebulun and Benjamin; [4] Dan and Naphtali; Gad and Asher. [5] The total number of Jacob's direct descendants was seventy. Joseph was already in Egypt. [6] Now Joseph and all his brothers and that whole generation died. [7] But the Israelites were fruitful and prolific. They multiplied and became so very numerous that the land was filled with them. [8] Then a new king, who knew nothing of Joseph, rose to power in Egypt. [9] He said to his people, "See! The Israelite people have multiplied and become more numerous than we are! [10] Come, let us deal shrewdly with them to stop their increase; otherwise, in time of war they too may join our enemies to fight against us, and so leave the land." (Exodus 1:1-10)

[14] Then the Lord said to Moses: Write this down in a book as something to be remembered and recite it to Joshua: I will completely blot out the memory of Amalek from under the heavens. (Exodus 17:14)

[4] Moses then wrote down all the words of the Lord and, rising early in the morning, he built at the foot of the mountain an altar and twelve sacred stones[a] for the twelve tribes of Israel. (Exodus 24:4)

The Discovery of Moses

By Julius Schnorr von Carolsfeld (Die Bibel in Bildern 1852-1860)

[1] Now a man of the house of Levi married a Levite woman, [2] and the woman conceived and bore a son. Seeing what a fine child he was, she hid him for three months. [3] But when she could no longer hide him, she took a papyrus basket, daubed it with bitumen and pitch, and putting the child in it, placed it among the reeds on the bank of the Nile. [4] His sister stationed herself at a distance to find out what would happen to him. (Exodus 2:1-4)

II. God's Deliverance of Israel (ch3-18)

Various routes of escape have been speculated, a northern route through the land of the Philistines, a middle route toward the east across Sinai to Beersheba, and a southern route along the west of Sinai to the southeast of the peninsula. The southern route seems most likely, although the exact place where the Israelites crossed the Red Sea is uncertain. Aside from the story of escape from Egypt through the dessert and into the promised land, the Book of Exodus does much more. It also lays the foundation for a theology of the God of Israel. His name is revealed, his attributes known, his redemption told, his law explained, and how he is to be worshiped. The book designates Moses' appointment as the mediator of the Mosaic covenant between God and the people of Israel given to him at Mount Sinai. It also describes how the priesthood in Judaism began and defines the role of the prophet in the religion. It instructs how the ancient Sinaitic covenant relationship between God and his people should be maintained and honored. Insights into the nature of God are also found in the Book of Exodus. Much focus is put on the importance of God's presence and glory living among his people. Emphasis is placed on attributes such as justice, truthfulness, mercy, faithfulness and holiness.

[13] *"But," said Moses to God, "if I go to the Israelites and say to them, 'The God of your ancestors has sent me to you,' and they ask me, 'What is his name?' what do I tell them?"* [14] *God replied to Moses: I am who I am. Then he added: This is what you will tell the Israelites: I AM has sent me to you.* [15] *God spoke further to Moses: This is what you will say to the Israelites: The Lord, the God of your ancestors, the God of Abraham, the God of Isaac, and the God of Jacob, has sent me to you. This is my name forever; this is my title for all generations. (Exodus 3:13-15)*

***

In the covenant between God and Moses Yahweh clearly defines the blessings and curses that may result if the covenant is broken.

[10] When the Lord, your God, brings you into the land which he swore to your ancestors, to Abraham, Isaac, and Jacob, that he would give you, a land with fine, large cities that you did not build, [11] with houses full of goods of all sorts that you did not garner, with cisterns that you did not dig, with vineyards and olive groves that you did not plant; and when, therefore, you eat and are satisfied, [12] be careful not to forget the Lord, who brought you out of the land of Egypt, that house of slavery. [13] The Lord, your God, shall you fear; him shall you serve, and by his name shall you swear. [14] You shall not go after other gods, any of the gods of the surrounding peoples— [15] for the Lord, your God who is in your midst, is a passionate God—lest the anger of the Lord, your God, flare up against you and he destroy you from upon the land. [16] You shall not put the Lord, your God, to the test, as you did at Massah. [17] But keep the commandments of the Lord, your God, and the decrees and the statutes he has commanded you. [18] Do what is right and good in the sight of the Lord, that it may go well with you, and you may enter in and possess the good land which the Lord promised on oath to your ancestors, [19] driving all your enemies out of your way, as the Lord has promised. (Exodus 6:10-19)

Moses is Sent to Egypt

By Julius Schnorr von Carolsfeld (Die Bibel in Bildern 1852-1860)

[7] But the Lord said: I have witnessed the affliction of my people in Egypt and have heard their cry against their taskmasters, so I know well what they are suffering. [8] Therefore I have come down[⌐] to rescue them from the power of the Egyptians and lead them up from that land into a good and spacious land, a land flowing with milk and honey, the country of the Canaanites, the Hittites, the Amorites, the Perizzites, the Girgashites, the Hivites and the Jebusites. [9] Now indeed the outcry of the Israelites has reached me, and I have seen how the Egyptians are oppressing them. [10] Now, go! I am sending you to Pharaoh to bring my people, the Israelites, out of Egypt. (Exodus 3:7-10)

Ten Plagues of Egypt:

The ten plagues of Egypt are described throughout chapters seven to twelve in Exodus. The Bible does not specifically say how long the plagues lasted, but consensus estimate that it was under one year. Moses was eighty years old when the ten plagues began. The Israelites wandered in the desert for forty years and Moses died at the end of the forty years at the age of 120 years old, the plagues would have had to end in under a year. The plagues served to contrast the power of the God of Israel with the Egyptian gods. With Egypt a world power at that time, this victory greatly strengthened the faith of the Israelites. The power and might of God was clearly demonstrated.

1) **Water into Blood:** *[20] Moses and Aaron did just as the Lord had commanded. He raised his staff in the presence of Pharaoh and his officials and struck the water of the Nile, and all the water was changed into blood. [21] The fish in the Nile died, and the river smelled so bad that the Egyptians could not drink its water. Blood was everywhere in Egypt. (Exodus 7:20-21)*

2) **The Frogs:** *[5] Then the Lord said to Moses, "Tell Aaron, 'Stretch out your hand with your staff over the streams and canals and ponds, and make frogs come up on the land of Egypt.'" [6] So Aaron stretched out his hand over the waters of Egypt, and the frogs came up and covered the land. [7] But the magicians did the same things by their secret arts; they also made frogs come up on the land of Egypt. (Exodus 8:5-7)*

3) **The Gnats:** *[12] Thereupon the Lord spoke to Moses: Speak to Aaron: Stretch out your staff and strike the dust of the earth, and it will turn into gnats throughout the land of Egypt. [13] They did so. Aaron stretched out his hand with his staff and struck the dust of the earth, and gnats came upon human being and beast alike. All the dust of the earth turned into gnats throughout the land of Egypt. (Exodus 8:12-13)*

4) **The Flies:** *¹⁷ For if you do not let my people go, I will send swarms of flies upon you and your servants and your people and your houses. The houses of the Egyptians and the very ground on which they stand will be filled with swarms of flies. ¹⁸ But on that day, I will make an exception of the land of Goshen, where my people are, and no swarms of flies will be there, so that you may know that I the Lord am in the midst of the land. (Exodus 8:17-18)*

5) **Diseased livestock:** *¹ Then the Lord said to Moses: Go to Pharaoh and tell him: Thus, says the LORD, the God of the Hebrews: Let my people go to serve me. ² For if you refuse to let them go and persist in holding them, ³ the hand of the Lord will strike your livestock in the field—your horses, donkeys, camels, herds and flocks—with a very severe pestilence. ⁴ But the Lord will distinguish between the livestock of Israel and that of Egypt, so that nothing belonging to the Israelites will die. (Exodus 9:1-4)*

6) **The Boils:** *⁸ So the Lord said to Moses and Aaron: Each of you take handfuls of soot from a kiln, and in the presence of Pharaoh let Moses scatter it toward the sky. ⁹ It will turn into fine dust over the whole land of Egypt and cause festering boils on human being and beast alike throughout the land of Egypt. ¹⁰ So they took the soot from a kiln and appeared before Pharaoh. When Moses scattered it toward the sky, it caused festering boils on human being and beast alike. (Exodus 9:8-10)*

7) **Thunderstorm of Hail and Fire:** *¹⁵ For by now I should have stretched out my hand and struck you and your people with such pestilence that you would have vanished from the earth. ¹⁶ But this is why I have let you survive: to show you my power and to make my name resound throughout the earth! ¹⁷ Will you continue to exalt yourself over my people and not let them go? ¹⁸ At this time tomorrow, therefore, I am going to rain down such fierce hail as there has never been in Egypt from the day it was founded up to the present. (Exodus 9:15-18)*

8) **The Locusts:** *³ So Moses and Aaron went to Pharaoh and told him, "Thus says the Lord, the God of the Hebrews: How long will you refuse to submit to me? Let my people go to serve me. ⁴ For if you refuse to let my people go, tomorrow I will bring locusts into your territory. ⁵ They will cover the surface of the earth, so that the earth itself will not be visible. They will eat up the remnant you saved undamaged from the hail, as well as all the trees that are growing in your fields. ⁶ They will fill your houses and the houses of your servants and of all the Egyptians—something your parents and your grandparents have not seen from the day they appeared on this soil until today." With that he turned and left Pharaoh. (Exodus 10:3-6)*

9) **Three Days of Darkness:** *²¹ Then the Lord said to Moses: Stretch out your hand toward the sky, that over the land of Egypt there may be such darkness that one can feel it. ²² So Moses stretched out his hand toward the sky, and there was dense darkness throughout the land of Egypt for three days. ²³ People could not see one another, nor could they get up from where they were, for three days. But all the Israelites had light where they lived. (Exodus 10:21-23)*

10) **Death of Firstborn:** *⁵ Every firstborn in the land of Egypt will die, from the firstborn of Pharaoh who sits on his throne to the firstborn of the slave-girl who is at the handmill, as well as all the firstborn of the animals, ⁶ Then there will be loud wailing throughout the land of Egypt, such as has never been, nor will ever be again. ⁷ But among all the Israelites, among human beings and animals alike, not even a dog will growl, so that you may know that the Lord distinguishes between Egypt and Israel. (Exodus 11:5-7)*

The Origin of the Paschal Lamb

By Julius Schnorr von Carolsfeld (Die Bibel in Bildern 1852-1860)

[21] Moses summoned all the elders of Israel and said to them, "Go and procure lambs for your families, and slaughter the Passover victims. [22] Then take a bunch of hyssop and dipping it in the blood that is in the basin, apply some of this blood to the lintel and the two doorposts. And none of you shall go outdoors until morning. [23] For when the Lord goes by to strike down the Egyptians, seeing the blood on the lintel and the two doorposts, the Lord will pass over that door and not let the destroyer come into your houses to strike you down. (Exodus 12:21-23)

The Egyptians Drown in the Red Sea

By Julius Schnorr von Carolsfeld (Die Bibel in Bildern 1852-1860)

[19] When Pharaoh's horses and chariots and horsemen entered the sea, the Lord made the waters of the sea flow back upon them, though the Israelites walked on dry land through the midst of the sea. [20] Then the prophet Miriam, Aaron's sister, took a tambourine in her hand, while all the women went out after her with tambourines, dancing; [21] and she responded to them: Sing to the Lord, for he is gloriously triumphant; horse and chariot he has cast into the sea. (Exodus 15:19-21)

God Gives Israel Bread and Water in the Desert
By Julius Schnorr von Carolsfeld (Die Bibel in Bildern 1852-1860)

⁴ Then the Lord said to Moses: I am going to rain down bread from heaven for you. Each day the people are to go out and gather their daily portion; thus will I test them, to see whether they follow my instructions or not. ⁵ On the sixth day, however, when they prepare what they bring in, let it be twice as much as they gather on the other days. ⁶ So Moses and Aaron told all the Israelites, "At evening you will know that it was the Lord who brought you out of the land of Egypt; ⁷ and in the morning, you will see the glory of the Lord, when he hears your grumbling against him. But who are we that you should grumble against us?" (Exodus 16:4-7)

III. Covenant at Sinai (ch19-24)

The Covenant of Moses:

The covenant at Sinai is just another step in God's fulfillment of his promise to the patriarchs as he had promised in Genesis. No affliction, no famine, or no battling enemy were outside the power of his control, and the pharaoh, the Egyptians and other groups saw the power of God and feared the Israelites. But the Biblical message of salvation and availability for redemption is also set forth in this book.

⁶Therefore, say to the Israelites: I am the Lord. I will free you from the burdens of the Egyptians and will deliver you from their slavery. I will redeem you by my outstretched arm and with mighty acts of judgment. (Exodus 6:6)

¹³In your love you led the people you redeemed; in your strength you guided them to your holy dwelling. (Exodus 15:13)

The heart of redemption theology is found in the Passover narrative of chapter twelve, the sealing of the covenant in chapter twenty-four, and the account of God's grace and renewal of that covenant after Israel's blatant unfaithfulness to it in their worship of the golden calf.

The foundation of Biblical ethics and morality is laid out in the character of God as revealed in the Ten Commandments of the Book of the Covenant, which taught how to apply the principles of the commandments. In the covenant between God and Moses Yahweh is clearly the Suzerain and Moses the vassal-lord who represents the people under the Suzerain authority.

***

[1] Then God spoke all these words: [2] I am the Lord your God, who brought you out of the land of Egypt, out of the house of slavery. [3] You shall not have other gods beside me. [4] You shall not make for yourself an idol or a likeness of anything in the heavens above or on the earth below or in the waters beneath the earth; [5] you shall not bow down before them or serve them. For I, the Lord, your God, am a jealous God, inflicting punishment for their ancestors' wickedness on the children of those who hate me, down to the third and fourth generation; [6] but showing love down to the thousandth generation of those who love me and keep my commandments. [7] You shall not invoke the name of the Lord, your God, in vain. For the Lord will not leave unpunished anyone who invokes his name in vain. [8] Remember the sabbath day—keep it holy. [9] Six days you may labor and do all your work, [10] but the seventh day is a sabbath of the Lord your God. You shall not do any work, either you, your son or your daughter, your male or female slave, your work animal, or the resident alien within your gates. [11] For in six days the LORD made the heavens and the earth, the sea and all that is in them; but on the seventh day he rested. That is why the Lord has blessed the sabbath day and made it holy. [12] Honor your father and your mother, that you may have a long life in the land the Lord your God is giving you. [13] You shall not kill. [14] You shall not commit adultery. [15] You shall not steal. [16] You shall not bear false witness against your neighbor. [17] You shall not covet your neighbor's house. You shall not covet your neighbor's wife, his male or female slave, his ox or donkey, or anything that belongs to your neighbor. (Exodus 20:1-17)

[22] The Lord said to Moses: This is what you will say to the Israelites: You have seen for yourselves that I have spoken to you from heaven. [23] You shall not make alongside of me gods of silver, nor shall you make for yourselves gods of gold. [24] An altar of earth make for me, and sacrifice upon it your burnt offerings and communion sacrifices, your sheep and your oxen. In every place where I cause my name to be invoked I will come to you and bless you. (Exodus 20:22-24)

The book concludes with the theology of worship and God's royal tent in Israel. God is not only mighty on Israel's behalf, but He is also present in the lives of the people. They are accountable to raising up Moses to liberate his people from Egyptian bondage, to bring them into a special covenant with Him, and to erect in his honor a royal tent to the God of Israel for worship.

¹ Then the Lord said to Moses: ² On the first day of the first month[a] you shall set up the tabernacle of the tent of meeting. ³ Put the ark of the covenant in it, and screen off the ark with the veil. ⁴ Bring in the table and set it. Then bring in the menorah and set up the lamps on it. ⁵ Put the golden altar of incense in front of the ark of the covenant and hang the curtain at the entrance of the tabernacle. ⁶ Put the altar for burnt offerings in front of the entrance of the tabernacle of the tent of meeting. ⁷ Place the basin between the tent of meeting and the altar and put water in it. ⁸ Set up the court round about and put the curtain at the gate of the court. ⁹ Take the anointing oil and anoint the tabernacle and everything in it, consecrating it and all its furnishings, so that it will be sacred. ¹⁰ Anoint the altar for burnt offerings and all its utensils, consecrating it, so that it will be most sacred. ¹¹ Likewise, anoint the basin with its stand, and thus consecrate it. ¹² Then bring Aaron and his sons to the entrance of the tent of meeting, and there wash them with water. ¹³ Clothe Aaron with the sacred vestments and anoint him, thus consecrating him as my priest. ¹⁴ Bring forward his sons also and clothe them with the tunics. ¹⁵ As you have anointed their father, anoint them also as my priests. Thus, by being anointed, shall they receive a perpetual priesthood throughout all future generations. ¹⁶ Moses did just as the Lord commanded him. (Exodus 40:1-16)

Moses Receives God's Ten Commandments

By Julius Schnorr von Carolsfeld (Die Bibel in Bildern 1852-1860)

¹ Then God spoke all these words: ² I am the Lord your God, who brought you out of the land of Egypt, out of the house of slavery. ³ You shall not have other gods beside me. ⁴ You shall not make for yourself an idol or a likeness of anything[⸳] in the heavens above or on the earth below or in the waters beneath the earth; ⁵ you shall not bow down before them or serve them. For I, the Lord, your God, am a jealous God, inflicting punishment for their ancestors' wickedness on the children of those who hate me, down to the third and fourth generation; ⁶ but showing love down to the thousandth generation of those who love me and keep my commandments. (Exodus 20:1-6)

IV. God's Royal Tent in Israel (ch25-40)

Ark of the Covenant:

Tradition holds that the Ark of the Covenant is said to house the two stone tablets that the Ten Commandments were chiseled on by God and given to Moses on Mount Sinai. It also contained Aaron's rod and a pot of Manna. The ark was built at the foot of Mount Sinai about one year after leaving Egypt. The Book of Exodus includes specific instructions on how it was to be built. The Levites (tribe of Aaron) were designated to carry it and to maintain it. The ark was to always be carried ahead of the people during the exodus and later into every battle. Aaron is said to be the first high priest (kohen gadol) in Exodus, although earlier texts state that Enoch of the Antediluvian period was also known as a high priest.

[10] You shall make an ark of acacia wood, two and a half cubits long, one and a half cubits wide, and one and a half cubits high. [11] Plate it inside and outside with pure gold and put a molding of gold around the top of it. [12] Cast four gold rings and put them on the four supports of the ark, two rings on one side and two on the opposite side. [13] Then make poles of acacia wood and plate them with gold. [14] These poles you are to put through the rings on the sides of the ark, for carrying it; [15] they must remain in the rings of the ark and never be withdrawn. [16] In the ark you are to put the covenant which I will give you. [17] You shall then make a cover of pure gold, two and a half cubits long, and one and a half cubits wide. [18] Make two cherubim of beaten gold for the two ends of the cover; [19] make one cherub at one end, and the other at the other end, of one piece with the cover, at each end. [20] The cherubim shall have their wings spread out above, sheltering the cover with them; they shall face each other, with their faces looking toward the cover. [21] This cover you shall then place on top of the ark. In the ark itself you are to put the covenant which I will give you. (Exodus 25:10-21)

The Idolatry of the Golden Calf

By Julius Schnorr von Carolsfeld (Die Bibel in Bildern 1852-1860)

¹ When the people saw that Moses was delayed in coming down from the mountain, they gathered around Aaron and said to him, "Come, make us a god who will go before us; as for that man Moses who brought us out of the land of Egypt, we do not know what has happened to him. " ² Aaron replied, "Take off the golden earrings that your wives, your sons, and your daughters are wearing, and bring them to me." ³ So all the people took off their earrings and brought them to Aaron. ⁴ He received their offering, and fashioning it with a tool, made a molten calf. Then they cried out, "These are your gods, Israel, who brought you^l up from the land of Egypt." ⁵ On seeing this, Aaron built an altar in front of the calf and proclaimed, "Tomorrow is a feast of the Lord." (Exodus 32:1-5)

The Renewal of God's Covenant

By Julius Schnorr von Carolsfeld (Die Bibel in Bildern 1852-1860)

[30] On the next day Moses said to the people, "You have committed a grave sin. Now I will go up to the Lord; perhaps I may be able to make atonement for your sin." [31] So Moses returned to the Lord and said, "Ah, this people has committed a grave sin in making a god of gold for themselves! [32] Now if you would only forgive their sin! But if you will not, then blot me out of the book that you have written." The Lord answered Moses: Only the one who has sinned against me will I blot out of my book. [34] Now, go and lead the people where I have told you. See, my angel will go before you. When it is time for me to punish, I will punish them for their sin. (Exodus 32:30-34)

***

²⁷ Then the Lord said to Moses: Write down these words, for in accordance with these words I have made a covenant with you and with Israel. ²⁸ So Moses was there with the Lord for forty days and forty nights, without eating any food or drinking any water, and he wrote on the tablets the words of the covenant, the ten words. ²⁹ As Moses came down from Mount Sinai with the two tablets of the covenant in his hands, he did not know that the skin of his face had become radiant while he spoke with the Lord. ³⁰ When Aaron, then, and the other Israelites saw Moses and noticed how radiant the skin of his face had become, they were afraid to come near him. ³¹ Only after Moses called to them did Aaron and all the leaders of the community come back to him. Moses then spoke to them. ³² Later, all the Israelites came up to him, and he enjoined on them all that the Lord had told him on Mount Sinai. ³³ When Moses finished speaking with them, he put a veil over his face. ³⁴ Whenever Moses entered the presence of the Lord to speak with him, he removed the veil until he came out again. On coming out, he would tell the Israelites all that he had been commanded. ³⁵ Then the Israelites would see that the skin of Moses' face was radiant; so he would again put the veil over his face until he went in to speak with the Lord. (Exodus 34:27-35)

Temple History:

The Hebrew Bible canon primarily developed between the construction of the Second Temple in Jerusalem in 515BC and the destruction of it by the Romans in 70AD. According to the Hebrew Bible, the First Temple, also known as Solomon's Temple, was destroyed by Nebuchadnezzar II after the Babylonian Siege of Jerusalem of 597BC when many were taken and sent into exile to Babylon. It was later replaced with the Second Temple in the 6th century BC. Although modern sources may differ, the Hebrew Bible portrays the temple as being constructed under Solomon, King of the United Monarchy of Israel, with the Kingdom of Israel to the north and the Kingdom of Judah (including Jerusalem) in the south. It is thought that the First Temple lasted between 400-500 years with construction thought to be around 830BC and destruction about 420BC. It was dedicated to Yahweh and is said to have housed the Ark of the Covenant. It is argued that both temples stood on the footprint that today holds the Temple Mount in the Old City of Jerusalem. During the Second Temple period three distinct Jewish sects emerged, the Essenes, the Sadducees, and the Pharisees.

This sacred footprint of land is also claimed by Islam to have been the spot where the Prophet Muhammad is said to have ascended to heaven in the 7th century. Today two Muslim buildings of worship occupy the space, the al-Aqsa Mosque and the Dome of the Rock.

[1] In the four hundred and eightieth year after the Israelites went forth from the land of Egypt, in the fourth year of Solomon's reign over Israel, in the month of Ziv (the second month), he began to build the house of the Lord. [2] The house which King Solomon built for the Lord was sixty cubits long, twenty wide, and thirty high. [3] The porch in front of the nave of the house was twenty cubits from side to side along the width of the house, and ten cubits deep in front of the house. (I Kings 6:1-3)

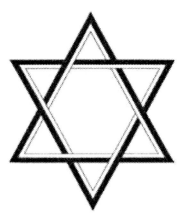

Chapter 4
The Book of Leviticus
(Vayikra / And He Called)
10 Parashot / 27 Chapters

Parashah	Hebrew	English	Chapter/Line
24	Vayikra	And He called	Leviticus 1:1-5:26
25	Tzav	Command	6:1-8:36
26	Shemini	Eighth	9:1-11:47
27	Tazria	She bears seed	12:1-13:59
28	Metzora	Infected one	14:1-15:33
29	Acharei Mot	After the death	16:1-18:30
30	Kedoshim	Holy ones	19:1-20:27
31	Emor	Say gently	21:1-24:23
32	Behar	On the Mount	25:1-26:2
33	Bechukotai	In My laws	26:3-27:34

***

The Book of Leviticus gets its name from the Septuagint, meaning *relating to the Levites*. Its Hebrew title, *wayyiqra*, is the first word in the Hebrew text of the book and means *and He called*. Although the book looks at more than the special duties of the Levites, it is named such because it is mainly directed to the service of worship at the tabernacle. This responsibility was held by the priests who were the sons of Aaron from the tribe of Levi. The Jewish sacrificial system of worship given to Moses was at the center and heart of all Jewish culture, as their government and their law was their religion.

This type of jurisprudence is similar to what occurred throughout Europe through the Middle Ages with the Catholic Church and is still found today in many areas of the Middle East with the Muslim religion. There are varying levels of practice from country to country, but eight countries still apply Muslim Sharia law in full, both in personal and criminal proceedings. In Africa, Mauritania and Sudan still maintain complete Sharia law; and in the Middle East, Saudi Arabia, Yemen, Iraq, Iran, Afghanistan, and Pakistan do.

As Exodus left us with directions for building the tabernacle, Leviticus left us with the laws and regulations for worshipping there. This includes instructions on cleanliness, ceremonial rituals, moral laws, holy days, the sabbath year and the Year of Jubilee. Tradition holds that these laws were revealed the year that the Israelites camped at Mount Sinai. At this time God directed Moses to organize worship, government, and military forces.

[5] The anointed priest shall then take some of the bull's blood and bring it into the tent of meeting, [6] where, dipping his finger in the blood, he shall sprinkle some of it seven times before the Lord, toward the veil of the sanctuary. (Leviticus 4:5-6)

I. The Five Main Offerings (chs1-7)

Burnt Offering:

The burnt offering was a sacrifice that was completely burnt. None of it was to be eaten at all, and therefore the fire consumed the whole sacrifice. The fire on the altar was to burn continuously. God is pleased to accept anyone who came to Him through this prescribed sacrifice. The animal was to atone for the sin of the person making the offering. This created fellowship between fellowship possible between a holy God and a sinful human.

³ If a person's offering is a burnt offering from the herd, the offering must be a male without blemish. The individual shall bring it to the entrance of the tent of meeting to find favor with the Lord, ⁴ and shall lay a hand on the head of the burnt offering, so that it may be acceptable to make atonement for the one who offers it. (Leviticus 1:3-4)

Grain Offering (Meal):

Cereal or vegetable could also be offered. Different grain preparations were stipulated, usually an offering of flour and oil in which the priest would take a portion along with incense to burn, then would eat the rest. It was considered a gift to God from the best of the produce in an attempt to have sins forgiven. A drink offering (libation) was poured on top of the grain as a symbol of joy.

⁴ When you offer a grain offering baked in an oven, it must be in the form of unleavened cakes made of bran flour mixed with oil, or of unleavened wafers spread with oil. (Leviticus 2:4)

Purification Offering (Sin):

This offering deals with forgiveness from unintentional sins and of cleansing *the tabernacle* of ceremonial uncleanness or human defilement. Each class of people had various ordinances to perform including the priest.

² Tell the Israelites: When a person inadvertently does wrong by violating any one of the Lord's prohibitions. ³ If it is the anointed priest who thus does wrong and thereby makes the people guilty, he shall offer to the Lord an unblemished bull of the herd as a purification offering for the wrong he committed. (Leviticus 4:2-3)

Guilt Offering (Reparation):

This offering intended for the sinner to at the damage the sin caused. It sought forgiveness, but the sinner had to pay full restitution.

¹⁶ The wrongdoer shall also restore what has been misused of the sacred objects, adding a fifth of its value, and give this to the priest. Thus, the priest shall make atonement for the person with the ram of the reparation offering, so that the individual may be forgiven. (Leviticus 5:16)

Peace Offering:

Unlike the other offerings, the peace offering is optional, and was in addition to the burnt offering. It is like the burnt offering, but rather than burning the animal to ashes, it was cooked and eaten with the priest, who represented the Lord. There were three primary peace offerings; the thanksgiving offering (act of thanks), a wave offering (priest would wave the offering before the Lord), and the votive offering (vow taken, a favor).

⁵ The priest shall burn these on the altar as an oblation to the Lord. It is a reparation offering. ⁶ Every male of the priestly line may eat of it; but it must be eaten in a sacred place. It is most holy. (Leviticus 7:5-6)

II. Installation and Ministry of Aaron & Sons (chs8-10)

Aaron, Miriam, and Moses were born to Amram, son of Kehath the Levite, who entered Egypt with Jacob's household, and Jochebed, the daughter of Levi. Aaron is considered the first high priest of Israel and his family had the responsibility to make offerings on the altar to the God of Israel. The rest of the Levites tribe were given subordinate responsibilities within the sanctuary. Aaron married Elisheba, daughter of Amminadab and sister of Nahshon of the tribe of Judah. The sons of Aaron were Eleazar, Ithamar, and Nadab and Abihu. Aaron died before the Israelites crossed the North Jordan river and was buried on Mount Hor.

[1] The Lord said to Moses: [2] Take Aaron along with his sons, the vestments, the anointing oil, the bull for a purification offering, the two rams, and the basket of unleavened bread, [3] then assemble the whole community at the entrance of the tent of meeting. [4] Moses did as the Lord had commanded. When the community had assembled at the entrance of the tent of meeting. [5] Moses told them: "This is what the Lord has ordered to be done." [6] Bringing forward Aaron and his sons, Moses first washed them with water. [7] Then he put the tunic on Aaron, girded him with the sash, clothed him with the robe, placed the ephod on him, and girded him with the ephod's embroidered belt, fastening the ephod on him with it. [8] He then set the breastpiece on him, putting the Urim and Thummim in it. [9] He put the turban on his head, attaching the gold medallion, the sacred headband, on the front of the turban, as the Lord had commanded Moses to do. (Leviticus 8:1-9)

III. Distinction Between Clean and Unclean (chs11-15)

⁴⁴ For I, the Lord, am your God. You shall make and keep yourselves holy, because I am holy. You shall not make yourselves unclean, then, by any swarming creature that crawls on the ground. (Leviticus 11:44)

A *theocracy* developed after the covenant at Sinai, which is a form of government that honors a deity as the source from which all authority derives. Israel became the earthly representation of God's kingdom on earth. Religious ritual became excessive, and sacrifices could only be offered at approved sanctuaries which were controlled by the priests. Since the priests determined what is considered pure and dictated to the people the meaning of the law, they maintained much control over the people.

²⁸ When she becomes clean from her flow, she shall count seven days; after this she becomes clean. ²⁹ On the eighth day she shall take two turtledoves or two pigeons and bring them to the priest at the entrance of the tent of meeting. ³⁰ The priest shall offer one of them as a purification offering and the other as a burnt offering. Thus, shall the priest make atonement before the Lord for her because of her unclean flow. (Leviticus 15:28-30)

IV. The Annual Day of Atonement (ch16)

Jewish Holidays:

The Jewish holidays occur on the same dates every year in the Hebrew calendar, however the dates vary in the Gregorian. This is because the difference in the Hebrew and Gregorian calendars, with the former based on both moon and sun, and the later based only on the sun. Tishrei is the first month of the civil year and the seventh month of the ecclesiastical year. It is the most important month for religious Jewish holidays. It falls in autumn, usually between September to October in the Gregorian calendar and is 30 days in length. *Rosh Hashanah* is on the first day of Tishrei. *Yom Kippur* is on the tenth day of Tishrei.

Rosh Hashanah is the traditional Jewish New Year which is referred to in the Bible as the Feast of Trumpets and in the Mishnah as the Day of Judgement. Traditionally it commemorates the creation, specifically the creation of man on the sixth day. Yom Kippur, also called the Day of Atonement, is ten days after Rosh Hashanah. In biblical times this was the only day of the year that the high priest could enter the inner sanctuary of the Temple Tabernacle where God dwelt. This sacred place was also called the Holy of Holies and said to contain the Ark of the Covenant that God ordered Moses to have built. The ark housed the Ten Commandments chiseled in stone that was given to Moses on Mount Sinai. Today it is speculated that the Dome of the Rock sits on the site.

The first ten days of Tishrei is known as the Ten Days of Repentance. During this time an examination of conscience, prayer, and fasting is performed, similar to the forty-day Lenten season for Christians. In Leviticus chapter sixteen, it is described how the high priest would take two goats, one would be sent into the wilderness to carry out the sins of the tribe and the other would be sacrificed on the alter with its blood sprinkled on the ark of the covenant. This religious ritual made atonement for the whole nation of Israel.

The word atonement is often equated with reconciliation, in this sense it would be a reconciliation of the Hebrews to their God, Jehovah. This practice is where the concept of scapegoat originated from in modern times. Other cultures at that time also practiced this ritual, some substituting people for the goats, those most marginalized and expendable in society. With the destruction of the Second Temple in 70 AD, the focus shifted from the Holy Space to Holy Time with holiday celebrations.

The Jewish holiday of Hanukkah (Festival of Lights) is observed for eight nights beginning on the 25th day of Kislev which occurs from late November to late December in the Gregorian calendar. It honors the successful revolt against the Seleucid Empire led by Judah Maccabee, a Jewish priest. Although it is considered a minor holiday, the Hanukkah menorah is recognized around the world as symbolic of the Jewish faith and tradition.

[17] No one else may be in the tent of meeting from the time he enters the inner sanctuary to make atonement until he departs. When he has made atonement for himself and his household, as well as for the whole Israelite assembly, [18] he shall come out to the altar before the Lord and purge it also. Taking some of the bull's and the goat's blood, he shall put it on the horns around the altar, [19] and with his finger sprinkle some of the blood on it seven times. Thus he shall purify it and sanctify it from the impurities of the Israelites. [20] When he has finished purging the inner sanctuary, the tent of meeting and the altar, Aaron shall bring forward the live goat. [21] Laying both hands on its head, he shall confess over it all the iniquities of the Israelites and their trespasses, including all their sins, and so put them on the goat's head. He shall then have it led into the wilderness by an attendant. [22] The goat will carry off all their iniquities to an isolated region. (Leviticus 16:17-22)

V. Holy Living (chs17-26)

Jewish Pilgrimage Festivals:

Three major Jewish festivals were commanded by the Torah in ancient Israel, *Pesach (Passover), Shavuot (Pentecost),* and *Sukkot (Tabernacles).* It was mandatory to travel to Jerusalem to participate in these festivities and ritual worship with the services of the high priests (kohanim). Passover (Pesach) is a spring festival which during the existence of the Temple in Jerusalem was connected to the offering of the first-fruits of the barley to be harvested. The holiday commemoration of their liberation by God from slavery in ancient Egypt and their freedom as a nation under the leadership of Moses. It commemorates the story of the Exodus as described in the Hebrew Bible, especially in the Book of Exodus, in which the Israelites were freed from slavery in Egypt. It occurs on the 15th day of the Hebrew month of Nisan which is seventh month of the civil year, which coincides with the Christian season of Lent. Shavuot, also called the Feast of Weeks is comparable to the Christian Passover. It is one of three pilgrimage festivals. It marks the wheat harvest in Israel and it commemorates the anniversary of the day God gave the Torah to the entire nation of Israel assembled at Mount Sinai. It is one of the three pilgrimage festivals in the Torah. Different from other holidays, the date for Shavuot is not explicitly fixed in the Torah. Sukkot is translated as Feast of Tabernacles or Feast of the Ingathering, meaning Feast of Booths. It is celebrated on the 15th day of the seventh month, Tishrei, in the autumn. Sukkot is agricultural and celebrates the year's end.

26 The Lord said to Moses: 27 Now the tenth day of this seventh month is the Day of Atonement. You will have a declared holy day. You shall humble yourselves and offer an oblation to the Lord. 28 On this day you shall not do any work, because it is the Day of Atonement, when atonement is made for you before the Lord, your God. (Leviticus 23:26-28)

VI. *Regulations for Offerings Vowed to the Lord (ch27)*

Leviticus explains how to be holy and to worship God in a holy manner. Holiness in this sense means to become separated from sin and to live exclusively for the Lord's purpose and glory. The primary focus of the book is on spiritual holiness to God and his people. Spiritual holiness is symbolized by physical perfection, therefore, instructions specify that only perfect animals are to be used for sacrifice. It also requires that priests cannot be with any deformity. This includes a woman's menstruating or discharge after giving birth, sores, burns, baldness, or any bodily discharge. Any lack of perfection may symbolize human spiritual defect, which can break spiritual wholeness. Those who have blemish can be banished from the camp until they are cured and examined again by the priests.

[1] The Lord said to Moses: [2] Speak to the Israelites and tell them: When anyone makes a vow to the Lord with respect to the value of a human being, [3] the value for males between the ages of twenty and sixty shall be fifty silver shekels, by the sanctuary shekel; [4] and for a female, the value shall be thirty shekels. [5] For persons between the ages of five and twenty, the value for a male shall be twenty shekels, and for a female, ten shekels. [6] For persons between the ages of one month and five years, the value for a male shall be five silver shekels, and for a female, three shekels. [7] For persons of sixty or more, for a male the value shall be fifteen shekels, and ten shekels for a female. [8] However, if the one who made the vow is too poor to meet the sum, the person must be set before the priest, who shall determine a value; the priest will do this in keeping with the means of the one who made the vow. (Leviticus 27:1-8)

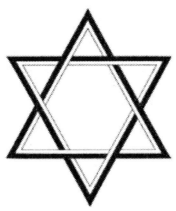

Chapter 5
The Book of Numbers
(Bemidbar / In the Wilderness)
10 Parashot / 36 Chapters

Parashah	Hebrew	English	Chapter/Line
34	Bamidbar	In the wilderness	Numbers 1:1-4:20
35	Naso	Elevate	4:21-7:89
36	Behaalotecha	In your uplifting	8:1-12:16
37	Shlach	Send for yourself	13:1-15:41
38	Korach	Korach	16:1-18:32
39	Chukat	Law	19:1-22:1
40	Balak	Balak	22:2-25:9
41	Pinchas	Phinehas	25:10-30:1
42	Matot	Tribes	30:2-32:42
43	Masei	Journeys of	33:1-36:13

***

The Book of Numbers gets its name from the Septuagint and is based on the two census lists that are found in chapters one and twentysix. The Hebrew title of the book, *bemidbar,* meaning *in the desert,* is more descriptive of the text. The book includes an account of the 38-year period of the Israelite's experience in the desert following the covenant on Mount Sinai. It continues the history of the move from Sinia to Canaan. It relates the story of Israel's journey from Mount Sinai to the plains of Moab on the border of Canaan. The book exposes talk of rebellion amoung God's people, their lack of obedience and their fall from faith. Because of this their judgment gets twarted and acts of rebellian are repeated. Some even refused to undertake the conquest of Cannan. The people forfeited their part in the promised land and were condemned to live out their lives in the desert. Only their children would enjoy the beauty and abundance of the promised land of Cannan that had originally been offered to them.

1st Census: *[1] In the second year after the Israelites' departure from the land of Egypt, on the first day of the second month, the Lord said to Moses at the tent of meeting in the wilderness of Sinai: [2] Take a census of the whole community of the Israelites, by clans and ancestral houses, registering by name each male individually. [3] You and Aaron shall enroll in companies all the men in Israel of twenty years or more who are fit for military service. (Numbers 1:1-3)*

2nd Census: *[1] the Lord said to Moses and Eleazar, son of Aaron the priest: [2] Take a census, by ancestral houses, throughout the community of the Israelites of all those of twenty years or more who are eligible for military service in Israel. [3] So on the plains of Moab along the Jordan at Jericho, Moses and Eleazar the priest enrolled them, [4] those of twenty years or more, as the Lord had commanded Moses. (Numbers 26:1-4)*

I. Preparing to Depart for Promised Land (1:1-10:10)

As the book begins the Lord organizes Israel into a military camp. In leaving Sinai, they march forward as his conquering army, with the Lord leading the way to establish his kingdom in the promised land. The narrative portrays Israel's identity as the Lord's redeemed people and the covenent made bween God and his favored servant people of God, charged with establishing his kingdom on earth. The Israelites celebrate the second passover one year after the exit from Egypt.

[1] A year after Israel's departure from Egypt, the Lord spoke to Moses in the wilderness of Sinai. In the first month of that year he said, [2] "Tell the Israelites to celebrate the Passover at the prescribed time, [3] at twilight on the fourteenth day of the first month. Be sure to follow all my decrees and regulations concerning this celebration." [4] So Moses told the people to celebrate the Passover [5] in the wilderness of Sinai as twilight fell on the fourteenth day of the month. And they celebrated the festival there, just as the Lord had commanded Moses. (Numbers 9:1-5)

II. The Journey from Sinai to Kadesh (10:11-12:16)

From the Book of Exodus the birth parents of Moses is revealed, and Miriam and Aaron as his birth siblings. Both are dedicated to Moses and his mission.

20 Amram married his aunt Jochebed, who bore him Aaron, Moses, and Miriam. Amram lived one hundred and thirty-seven years. 21 (Exodus 6:20)

But conflict is exposed in the Book of Numbers. Both Miriam and Aaron express displeasure with Moses wife, Zipporah, because she is from Midia and has a Cushite ethnic background. Discouragement leads to complaints and rebellion and God's actions are disclosed against his disobedient people. God sends a plague. The fourth book of the Pentateuch presents a sad reality that the God who had entered into covenant with Abraham, who had delivered his people from bondage in the Exodus, and who had revealed his holiness, was also a God of wrath. Miriam is stricken with leaprosy, her punishment for disobediance and unfaithfulness to God.

10 Now the cloud withdrew from the tent, and there was Miriam, stricken with a scaly infection, white as snow! When Aaron turned toward Miriam and saw her stricken with snow-white scales, 11 he said to Moses, "Ah, my Lord! Please do not charge us with the sin that we have foolishly committed! 12 Do not let her be like the stillborn baby that comes forth from its mother's womb with its flesh half consumed." 13 Then Moses cried to the Lord, "Please, not this! Please, heal her!" 14 But the Lord answered Moses: Suppose her father had spit in her face, would she not bear her shame for seven days? Let her be confined outside the camp for seven days; afterwards she may be brought back. (Numbers 12:10-14)

Spies are Sent into Canaan

By Julius Schnorr von Carolsfeld (Die Bibel in Bildern 1852-1860)

[25] They returned from reconnoitering the land forty days later. [26] Proceeding directly to Moses and Aaron and the whole community of the Israelites in the wilderness of Paran at Kadesh, they made a report to them and to the whole community, showing them the fruit of the land. [27] They told Moses: "We came to the land to which you sent us. It does indeed flow with milk and honey, and here is its fruit. [28] However, the people who are living in the land are powerful, and the towns are fortified and very large. Besides, we saw descendants of the Anakim there. [29] Amalekites live in the region of the Negeb; Hittites, Jebusites and Amorites dwell in the highlands, and Canaanites along the sea and the banks of the Jordan." (Numbers 13:25-29)

III. Kadesh, Delay Resulting from Rebellion (13:1-20:13)

[1] The Israelites, the whole community, arrived in the wilderness of Zin in the first month, and the people stayed at Kadesh. It was here that Miriam died, and here that she was buried. [2] Since the community had no water, they held an assembly against Moses and Aaron. [3] The people quarreled with Moses, exclaiming, "Would that we had perished when our kindred perished before the Lord! [4] Why have you brought the Lord's assembly into this wilderness for us and our livestock to die here? [5] Why have you brought us up out of Egypt, only to bring us to this wretched place? It is not a place for grain nor figs nor vines nor pomegranates! And there is no water to drink!" [6] But Moses and Aaron went away from the assembly to the entrance of the tent of meeting, where they fell prostrate. (Numbers 20:1-6)

The passing of the old guard. Those whom God has used to establish the nation are dying before the nation has independently come into its own.

[22] Setting out from Kadesh, the Israelites, the whole community, came to Mount Hor. [23] There at Mount Hor, on the border of the land of Edom, the Lord said to Moses and Aaron: [24] Let Aaron be gathered to his people, for he shall not enter the land I have given to the Israelites, because you both rebelled against my directions at the waters of Meribah. [25] Take Aaron and Eleazar his son and bring them up on Mount Hor. [26] Then strip Aaron of his garments and put them on Eleazar, his son; but there Aaron shall be gathered up in death. [27] Moses did as the Lord commanded. When they had climbed Mount Hor in view of the whole community, [28] Moses stripped Aaron of his garments and put them on Eleazar his son. Then Aaron died there on top of the mountain. When Moses and Eleazar came down from the mountain, [29] all the community understood that Aaron had breathed his last; and for thirty days the whole house of Israel mourned Aaron. (Numbers 20:22-29)

IV. Journey from Kadesh to Plains of Moab (20:14-22:1)

Around 1400 BC, about 40 years after Kadesh, the Israelites begin to move north toward Canaan. They travel to the east of the River Jordan through the mountainous region past Zalmonah and Punon. They camp at Oboth and Iye Abarim and cross the valley of the River Zered to Moab.

[10] The Israelites moved on and encamped in Oboth. [11] Then they moved on from Oboth and encamped in Iye-abarim in the wilderness facing Moab on the east. [12] Moving on from there, they encamped in the Wadi Zered. [13] Moving on from there, they encamped on the other side of the Arnon, in the wilderness that extends from the territory of the Amorites; for the Arnon forms Moab's boundary, between Moab and the Amorites. [14] Hence it is said in the "Book of the Wars of the Lord": "Waheb in Suphah and the wadies, [15]Arnon and the wadi gorges That reach back toward the site of Ar and lean against the border of Moab." [16] From there they went to Beer, which is the well of which the Lord said to Moses, Gather the people together so that I may give them water. [17] Then Israel sang this song: Spring up, O well, so sing to it [18] The well that the princes sank, that the nobles of the people dug, With their scepters and their staffs—from the wilderness, a gift. [19] From Beer to Nabaliel, from Nahaliel to Bamoth, [20] from Bamoth to the valley in the country of Moab at the headland of Pisgah that overlooks Jeshimon. (Numbers 21:10-20)

God Sends Fiery Serpents

By Julius Schnorr von Carolsfeld (Die Bibel in Bildern 1852-1860)

⁶ So the Lord sent among the people seraph[a] serpents, which bit the people so that many of the Israelites died. ⁷ Then the people came to Moses and said, "We have sinned in complaining against the Lord and you. Pray to the Lord to take the serpents from us." So Moses prayed for the people, ⁸ and the Lord said to Moses: Make a seraph and mount it on a pole, and everyone who has been bitten will look at it and recover. ⁹ Accordingly Moses made a bronze serpent and mounted it on a pole, and whenever the serpent bit someone, the person looked at the bronze serpent and recovered. (Numbers 21:6-9)

V. Israel on the Plains of Moab / Appendixes (22:2-36:13)

The last chapters of Numbers portray the Israelites as attempting to enter the promised land. They easily destroy two nations that confront them as they are entering. King Balak of Moab attempts to have his prophet Balaam for the purpose of cursing the migrating Israelite community. He has Balaam to try to seduce the Israelites into worshiping Baal. Because of this disobedience, about 24,000 people die, including Balaam. Joshua assumes the leadership of Israel in place of Moses who is banned from the promise land, due to his disobedience. In chapter thirty-four the land boundaries are given.

3 Your southern boundary will be at the wilderness of Zin along the border of Edom; on the east your southern boundary will begin at the end of the Salt Sea. 4 Then your boundary will turn south of the Akrabbim Pass and cross Zin. Terminating south of Kadesh-barnea, it extends to Hazar-addar and crosses to Azmon. 5 Then the boundary will turn from Azmon to the Wadi of Egypt and terminate at the Sea. 6 For your western boundary you will have the Great Sea with its coast; this will be your western boundary. 7 This will be your boundary on the north: from the Great Sea you will draw a line to Mount Hor, 8 and draw it from Mount Hor to Lebo-hamath, with the boundary terminating at Zedad. 9 Then the boundary extends to Ziphron and terminates at Hazar-enan. This will be your northern boundary. 10 For your eastern boundary you will draw a line from Hazar-enan to Shepham. 11 From Shepham the boundary will go down to Riblah, east of Ain, and descending further, the boundary will strike the ridge on the east side of the Sea of Chinnereth; 12 then the boundary will descend along the Jordan and terminate with the Salt Sea. This will be your land, with the boundaries that surround it. (Numbers 34:3-12)

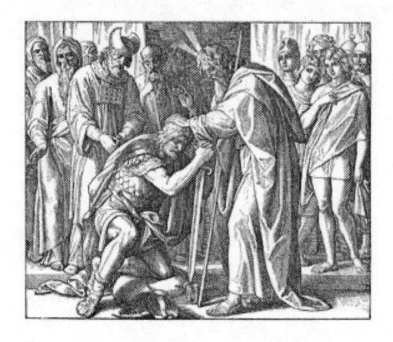

The Appointment of Joshua

By Julius Schnorr von Carolsfeld (Die Bibel in Bildern 1852-1860)

[15] Then Moses said to the Lord, [16] "May the Lord, the God of the spirits of all humanity, set over the community someone [17] who will be their leader in battle and who will lead them out and bring them in, that the Lord's community may not be like sheep without a shepherd." [18] And the Lord replied to Moses: Take Joshua, son of Nun, a man of spirit, and lay your hand upon him. [19] Have him stand before Eleazar the priest and the whole community, and commission him in their sight. [20] Invest him with some of your own power, that the whole Israelite community may obey him. [21] He shall present himself to Eleazar the priest, who will seek for him the decision of the Urim in the Lord's presence; and as it directs, Joshua, all the Israelites with him, and the whole community will go out for battle; and as it directs, they will come in. (Numbers 27:15-21)

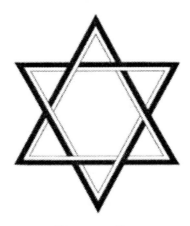

Chapter 6
The Book of Deuteronomy
(Devarim / Words)
11 Parashot / 34 Chapters

Parashah	Hebrew	English	Chapter/Line
44	Devarim	Words	Deuteronomy 1:1-3:22
45	Va'etchanan	Pleaded	3:23-7:11
46	Eikev	As a result	7:12-11:25
47	Re'eh	See	11:26-16:17
48	Shoftim	Judges	16:18-21:9
49	Ki Teitzei	When you go out	21:10-25:19
50	Ki Tavo	When you enter in	26:1-29:8
51	Nitzavim	Ones Standing	29:9-30:20
52	Vayelech	And he went	31:1-31:30
53	Haazinu	Listen	32:1-32:52
54	V'Zot HaBerachah	And this is the blessing	33:1-34:12

I. Preamble (1:1-5)

The Book of Deuteronomy places Moses and the Israelites in the territory of Moab at the point where the Jordan flows into the Dead Sea. In this book Moses reaffirms the laws that were especially important to him and speaks from the heart as a servant of God rather than the matter-of-fact style in Leviticus and Numbers. As his final act Moses transfers leadership to Joshua. He delivers his farewell address prior to preparing the people for their entrance into Canaan.

[1] These are the words that Moses spoke to all Israel beyond the Jordan in the wilderness, in the Arabah, opposite Suph, between Paran and Tophel, Laban, Hazeroth, and Dizahab. [2] It is a journey of eleven days from Horeb to Kadesh-barnea by way of the highlands of Seir. [3] In the fortieth year, on the first day of the eleventh month, Moses spoke to the Israelites according to all that the Lord had commanded him to speak to them, [4] after he had defeated Sihon, king of the Amorites, who reigned in Heshbon, and Og, king of Bashan, who reigned in Ashtaroth and in Edrei. [5] Beyond the Jordan, in the land of Moab, Moses undertook to explain this law: (Deuteronomy 1:1-5)

II. Historical Prologue (1:6-4:43)

[44] This is the law which Moses set before the Israelites. [45] These are the decrees, and the statutes and ordinances which Moses proclaimed to the Israelites after they came out of Egypt, [46] beyond the Jordan in the valley opposite Beth-peor, in the land of Sihon, king of the Amorites, who reigned in Heshbon, whom Moses and the Israelites defeated after they came out of Egypt. [47] They took possession of his land and the land of Og, king of Bashan, as well—the land of these two kings of the Amorites in the region beyond the Jordan to the east: [48] from Aroer on the edge of the Wadi Arnon to Mount Sion (that is, Hermon) [49] and all the Arabah beyond the Jordan to the east, as far as the Arabah Sea under the slopes of Pisgah. (Deuteronomy 4:44-49)

Judaism Today:

Main divisions of Judaism today are between the Orthodox, Conservative, Reconstructionist, and Reform movements. Until the late 18th century, Orthodox was the only kind of Judaism practiced. In this belief the Oral Torah was said to have been transmitted orally directly from God to Moses on Mount Sinai during the Exodus from Egypt. However, the differing Rabbinic groups today disagree on the divinity of the Oral Torah. The Jewish Enlightenment of the late 18th century called the *Haskalah* was an intellectual movement throughout Europe that opened the door for differing thoughts and denominations. But while the Conservative and Reform Jews show respect to the Oral Law and interpretation of the sages, they are also allowed to formulate and adopt their own rulings and interpretations. Beliefs concerning Jewish Law also separate the groups. Until the Haskalah, the collective body of Jewish religious laws derived from the Written and Oral Law. Halakha was universally required religious practice with all Jews. This remains the position among Orthodox and Conservative Jews, however Reconstructionist and Reform Judaism does not generally treat halakha as being binding today.

III. Stipulations of the Covenant (4:44-26:19)

⁶ I am the Lord your God, who brought you out of the land of Egypt, out of the house of slavery. ⁷ You shall not have other gods beside me. ⁸ You shall not make for yourself an idol or a likeness of anything in the heavens above or on the earth below or in the waters beneath the earth; ⁹ you shall not bow down before them or serve them. For I, the Lord, your God, am a jealous God, bringing punishment for their parents' wickedness on the children of those who hate me, down to the third and fourth generation, ¹⁰ but showing love down to the thousandth generation of those who love me and keep my commandments. ¹¹ You shall not invoke the name of the Lord, your God, in vain. For the Lord will not leave unpunished anyone who invokes his name in vain. ¹² Observe the sabbath day—keep it holy, as the·Lord, your God, commanded you. ¹³ Six days you may labor and do all your work, ¹⁴ but the seventh day is a sabbath of the Lord your God. You shall not do any work, either you, your son or your daughter, your male or female slave, your ox or donkey or any work animal, or the resident alien within your gates, so that your male and female slave may rest as you do. ¹⁵ Remember that you too were once slaves in the land of Egypt, and the Lord, your God, brought you out from there with a strong hand and outstretched arm. That is why the Lord, your God, has commanded you to observe the sabbath day. ¹⁶ Honor your father and your mother, as the Lord, your God, has commanded you, that you may have a long life and that you may prosper in the land the Lord your God is giving you. ¹⁷ You shall not kill. ¹⁸ You shall not commit adultery. ¹⁹ You shall not steal. ²⁰ You shall not bear dishonest witness against your neighbor. ²¹ You shall not covet your neighbor's wife. You shall not desire your neighbor's house or field, his male or female slave, his ox or donkey, or anything that belongs to your neighbor. (Deuteronomy 5:6-21)

IV. Ratification; Curses and Blessings (chs27-30)

In chapter twenty-seven of Deuteronomy the Israelites are given instructions to build an altar on Mount Ebal before crossing the River Jordan and entering the land promised to them. After this they are instructed to split into two groups; with one group to stay on Mount Ebal to pronounce curses, and the other to go to Mount Gerizim to pronounce blessings. The tribes of Reuben, Gad, Asher, Zebulun, Dan, and Naphtali were to stay on Mount Ebal. The tribes of Simeon, Levi, Judah, Issachar, Joseph, and Benjamin were sent to Mount Gerizim. The text goes on to list twelve curses, which were to be pronounced by the Levite priest and answered by the people with Amen. Blessings of victories and prosperity are promised for obedience. However, far more curses are threatened if the people do not follow God's laws. Sickness, defeat, oppression, exile, invasion, plagues, despoilment, etc. Chapter thirty talks about having compassion for the repentant and recaps the *choices* laid before the people to follow.

[19] I call heaven and earth today to witness against you: I have set before you life and death, the blessing and the curse. Choose life, then, that you and your descendants may live, [20] by loving the Lord, your God, obeying his voice, and holding fast to him. For that will mean life for you, a long life for you to live on the land which the Lord swore to your ancestors, to Abraham, Isaac, and Jacob, to give to them. (Deuteronomy 30:19-20)

V. Leadership Succession under Covenant (chs31-34)

[6] *"**Let Reuben live and not die**, nor his people be few."*

[7] *And this he said about Judah:*

"Hear, Lord, the cry of Judah; bring him to his people. With his own hands he defends his cause. Oh, be his help against his foes!"

[8] *About Levi he said:*

"Your Thummim and Urim belong to your faithful servant. You tested him at Massah; you contended with him at the waters of Meribah. [9] He said of his father and mother, 'I have no regard for them.' He did not recognize his brothers or acknowledge his own children, but he watched over your word and guarded your covenant. [10] He teaches your precepts to Jacob and your law to Israel. He offers incense before you and whole burnt offerings on your altar. [11] Bless all his skills, Lord, and be pleased with the work of his hands. Strike down those who rise against him, his foes till they rise no more."

[12] *About Benjamin he said:*

"Let the beloved of the Lord rest secure in him, for he shields him all day long, and the one the Lord loves rests between his shoulders."

[13] *About Joseph he said:*

"May the Lord bless his land with the precious dew from heaven above and with the deep waters that lie below; [14] with the best the sun brings forth and the finest the moon can yield; [15] with the choicest gifts of the ancient mountains and the fruitfulness of the everlasting hills; [16] with the best gifts of the earth and its fullness and the favor of him who dwelt in the burning bush. Let all these rest on the head of Joseph, on the brow of the prince among his brothers. [17] In majesty he is like a firstborn bull; his horns are the horns of a

wild ox. With them he will gore the nations, even those at the ends of the earth. Such are the ten thousand of Ephraim; such are the thousands of Manasseh."

¹⁸ **About Zebulun he said:**

"Rejoice, Zebulun, in your going out, and you, Issachar, in your tents. ¹⁹ They will summon peoples to the mountain and there offer the sacrifices of the righteous; they will feast on the abundance of the seas, on the treasures hidden in the sand."

²⁰ **About Gad he said:**

"Blessed is he who enlarges Gad's domain! Gad lives there like a lion, tearing at arm or head. ²¹ He chose the best land for himself; the leader's portion was kept for him. When the heads of the people assembled, he carried out the Lord's righteous will, and his judgments concerning Israel."

²² **About Dan he said:**

"Dan is a lion's cub, springing out of Bashan."

²³ **About Naphtali he said:**

"Naphtali is abounding with the favor of the Lord and is full of his blessing; he will inherit southward to the lake."

²⁴ **About Asher he said:**

"Most blessed of sons is Asher; let him be favored by his brothers and let him bathe his feet in oil. ²⁵ The bolts of your gates will be iron and bronze, and your strength will equal your days.

(Deuteronomy 33:6-25)

***

The word Deuteronomy, which means *repetition of the law*, arose from a mistranslation in the Septuagint, the pre-Christian Hebrew to Greek translation, which in Hebrew means *copy of this law*. The book is the last of the five books in the Pentateuch.

18 When he is sitting upon his royal throne, he shall write a copy of this law upon a scroll from the one that is in the custody of the Levitical priests. (Deuteronomy 17:18)

The story that unfolds in the first four books (Genesis, Exodus, Leviticus, Numbers) is an account of the journey of the Jewish people from the Creation, survival of the flood, escape from Egyptian enslavement, and through the desert journey to Canaan. As we later see in Joshua, the first of the Historical Books, closure eventually comes with the movement from promise to fulfillment. At the end of Numbers, Israel sits on the plains of Moab by the Jordan across from Jericho.

13 These are the commandments and decisions which the Lord commanded the Israelites through Moses, on the plains of Moab beside the Jordan opposite Jericho. (Numbers 36:13)

But in Deuteronomy, they are at a stand-still having little progression. And at the end of the book, the people are still there waiting to cross the Jordan.

8 The Israelites wept for Moses in the plains of Moab for thirty days, till they had completed the period of grief and mourning for Moses. 9 Now Joshua, son of Nun, was filled with the spirit of wisdom, since Moses had laid his hands upon him; and so the Israelites gave him their obedience, just as the Lord had commanded Moses. (Deuteronomy 34:8-9)

All that has happened is the transition from the ministry of Moses as God's chosen leader to that of Joshua named to replace him. Moses' final act as the Lord's appointed servant marks the end of the Pentateuch. The next Book of Joshua narrates the fulfillment of the promises made to the patriarchs in the Pentateuch and concludes the mission on which Moses had been sent. This also serves as the introduction to the Former Prophets, the first of the Historical Books.

¹ After Moses, the servant of the Lord, had died, the Lord said to Moses' aide Joshua, son of Nun: ² Moses my servant is dead. So now, you and the whole people with you, prepare to cross the Jordan to the land that I will give the Israelites. (Joshua 1:1-2)

Deuteronomy creates a long pause in the advancement of the story of redemption and deliverance from bondage in Egypt, a world power at that time. It tries so hard to advance to a place where Israel can be a free people under the rule of God; of freedom from fear in the post-Babel world to security in the promised land; and of deliverance from banishment from God's Garden to a life in the Lord's own land. However, it falls short and Moses never gets to see the land that God promised his ancestors.

The literary structure of Deuteronomy is common to its historical setting of the second millennium BC, which reflects the suzerain-vassal treaties of the Near Eastern state structures that emphasizes the covenant between the king's pledge to be suzerain and protector. In this situation, the Lord would be Israel's suzerain and protector if they would be faithful to him as their covenant Lord and obedient to the covenant stipulations as the vassal people of his kingdom. There would be blessings for such obedience, but curses for disobedience.

¹ Now, if you diligently obey the voice of the Lord, your God, carefully observing all his commandments which I give you today, the Lord, your God, will set you high above all the nations of the earth. ² All these blessings will come upon you and overwhelm you when you obey the voice of the Lord, your God: ³ May you be blessed in the city and blessed in the country! ⁴ Blessed be the fruit of your womb, the produce of your soil and the offspring of your livestock, the issue of your herds and the young of your flocks! ⁵ Blessed be your grain basket and your kneading bowl! ⁶ May you be blessed in your coming in and blessed in your going out! (Deuteronomy 28:1-6)

The purpose of the Book of Deuteronomy was to prepare the new generation of the chosen people to continue into the land that was promised to their ancestors in the Abrahamic covenant. It was to continue the relationship between the Lord and his people, the spiritual emphasis and its call to total commitment to the Lord in worship and obedience. The next book of the Former Prophets (Joshua, Judges, Samuel, Kings) continues with the style, themes and motifs of Deuteronomy.

Authorship of the Pentateuch/Torah:

As you can see below, both Old Testament and New Testament passages has ascribed Moses as the author of the first five books, although modern scholars have argued that there may have been more than one author.

⁷ Only be strong and steadfast, being careful to observe the entire law which Moses my servant enjoined on you. Do not swerve from it either to the right or to the left, that you may succeed wherever you go. ⁸ Do not let this book of the law depart from your lips. Recite it by day and by night, that you may carefully observe all that is written in it; then you will attain your goal; then you will succeed. (Joshua 1:7-8)

³ Keep the mandate of the Lord, your God, walking in his ways and keeping his statutes, commands, ordinances, and decrees as they are written in the law of Moses, that you may succeed in whatever you do, and wherever you turn, (1 Kings 2:3)

⁴ "Remember the law of Moses My servant, even the statutes and ordinances which I commanded him in Horeb for all Israel. (Malachi 4:4)

From Mark:

¹⁸ Some Sadducees, who say there is no resurrection, came to him and put this question to him, ¹⁹ saying, "Teacher, Moses wrote for us, 'If someone's brother dies, leaving a wife but no child, his brother must take the wife and raise up descendants for his brother.' (Mark 12:18-19)

From Stephen:

³⁷ It was this Moses who said to the Israelites, 'God will raise up for you, from among your own kinsfolk, a prophet like me.' ³⁸ It was he who, in the assembly in the desert, was with the angel who spoke to him on Mount Sinai and with our ancestors and received living utterances to hand on to us. (Acts 7:37-38)

From Peter:

¹⁹ Repent, therefore, and be converted, that your sins may be wiped away, ²⁰ and that the Lord may grant you times of refreshment and send you the Messiah already appointed for you, Jesus, ²¹ whom heaven must receive until the times of universal restoration of which God spoke through the mouth of his holy prophets from of old. ²² For Moses said: 'A prophet like me will the Lord, your God, raise up for you from among your own kinsmen; to him you shall listen in all that he may say to you. ²³ Everyone who does not listen to that prophet will be cut off from the people.' (Acts 3:19-23)

The Death of Moses

By Julius Schnorr von Carolsfeld (Die Bibel in Bildern 1852-1860)

[1] This is the blessing that Moses the man of God pronounced on the Israelites before his death. [2] He said: "The Lord came from Sinai and dawned over them from Seir; he shone forth from Mount Paran. He came with myriads of holy ones from the south, from his mountain slopes. [3] Surely it is you who love the people; all the holy ones are in your hand. At your feet they all bow down, and from you receive instruction, [4] the law that Moses gave us, the possession of the assembly of Jacob. [5] He was king over Jeshurun when the leaders of the people assembled, along with the tribes of Israel. (Deuteronomy 33:1-5)

Deuteronomy Conclusion:

The theme of the last book of the Pentateuch is much more than a list of rules, regulations, and laws to follow. The message here is to remind ourselves of the need to trust in God, to obey his commandments, and to treat others as you would like to be treated. It reminds us to resist the temptation of idolatry and the worshipping of false gods. And it cautions us that the constant pursuit of excessive wealth and materialism can eventually become false gods!

¹ Then Moses went up from the plains of Moab to Mount Nebo, the peak of Pisgah which faces Jericho, and the Lord showed him all the land—Gilead, and as far as Dan, ² all Naphtali, the land of Ephraim and Manasseh, all the land of Judah as far as the Western Sea, ³ the Negeb, the plain (the valley of Jericho, the City of Palms), and as far as Zoar. ⁴ The Lord then said to him, "This is the land about which I promised on oath to Abraham, Isaac, and Jacob, I will give it to your descendants. I have let you see it with your own eyes, but you shall not cross over." ⁵ So there, in the land of Moab, Moses, the servant of the Lord, died as the Lord had said; ⁶ and he was buried in a valley in the land of Moab, opposite Beth-peor; to this day no one knows the place of his burial. ⁷ Moses was one hundred and twenty years old when he died, yet his eyes were undimmed and his vigor unabated. ⁸ The Israelites wept for Moses in the plains of Moab for thirty days, till they had completed the period of grief and mourning for Moses. ⁹ Now Joshua, son of Nun, was filled with the spirit of wisdom, since Moses had laid his hands upon him; and so the Israelites gave him their obedience, just as the Lord had commanded Moses. ¹⁰ Since then no prophet has arisen in Israel like Moses, whom the Lord knew face to face, ¹¹ in all the signs and wonders the Lord sent him to perform in the land of Egypt against Pharaoh and all his servants and against all his land, ¹² and all the great might and the awesome power that Moses displayed in the sight of all Israel. (Deuteronomy 34:1-12)

Appendix I: List of Scripture and Schnorr Illustrations

Ch1 In the Beginning

Revealed Religion

Early Monotheism

(Exodus 7:11-12) (Exodus 12:12) (Exodus 20:3)

Holy Texts

Babylonian Exile

Essenes / Sadducees / Pharisees

Rabbinic Judaism and the Talmud:

Ch2 Book of Genesis

  (Genesis 15:6)

I. Creation (1:1-2:3)

  (Genesis 1:28-31)

Image001 The First Day of Creation (Genesis 1:1-5)

Image002 The Second Day of Creation (Genesis 1:6-8)

Image003 The Third Day of Creation (Genesis 1:9-13)

Image004 The Fourth Day of Creation (Genesis 1:14-19)

Babylonian Cultural Influence

Image005 The Fifth Day of Creation (Genesis 1:20-23)

Image006 The Sixth Day of Creation (Genesis 1:24-27)

II. Primeval History (2:4-11:26)

The Nephilim (Genesis 6:1-4)

Image007 The Sabbath (Genesis 2:2-3)

Suzerain Treaties and the Covenants

Image008 The Fall of Man (Genesis 3:2-7)

Image009 The First Judgement of God (Genesis 3:16-19)

Image010 The Expulsion from Eden (Genesis 3:22-24)

Image011 Adam and Eve After the Expulsion (Genesis 4:1-2)

Image012 Cain and Abel's Offering (Genesis 4:3-7)

Image013 Cain Kills His Brother Abel (Genesis 4:8-12)

Adam and Eve

Descendants of Cain and Seth (Genesis 4:17-26)

Image014 The Prophecy of the Flood (Genesis 6:9-13)

Image015 The Flood (Genesis 7:17-22)

Image016 The Ark Rests Upon Ararat (Genesis 8:1-5)

Covenant Theology

>(Titus 1:1-3)

>(Genesis 2:15-17)

>(Jeremiah 31:31-33)

>(Luke 22:19-20)

>(Hebrews 12:22-24)

>(2 Corinthians 3:5-6)

Dispensational Theology

Covenantal Theology

Image017 The Covenant of the Rainbow (Genesis 9:8-11)

Image018 The Tower of Babel (Genesis 11:1-4)

III. Patriarchal History (11:27-50:26)

Abram/Abraham (Genesis 25:5-6)

Abraham: Covenant of Circumcision (Genesis 17:1-14)

Image019 God's Promise to Abram (Genesis 12:1-3)

Image020 Abram Receives the First Promise (Genesis 12:7-9)

Ishmael

>(Genesis 16:3) / (Genesis 21:9-13)

>(Genesis 25:8-10) / (Genesis 25:13-18)

Image021 Abraham Receives God's Promise of a Son (Genesis 17:9-22)

Image022 The Sacrifice of Isaac (Genesis 22:15-19)

Isaac

>(Genesis 24:1-4)

>(Gen 25:19-23)

Image023 Rebekah Gives Abraham's Servant Water (Genesis 24:15-17)

Image024 Isaac Is Deceived by Jacob (Genesis 27:13-17)

Image025 Jacob's Dream (Genesis 28:10-14)

Image026 Jacob and Rachel at the Well (Genesis 29:9-12)

Jacob and Esau (Genesis 36:1-8) (Genesis 47:20-26)

Image027 Jacob Wrestles with the Angel (Genesis 32:23-29)

Image028 Jacob's Reconciliation with Esau (Genesis 32:4-7)

Image029 Joseph is Sold into Egypt (Genesis 37:28-33)

Image030 Joseph Interprets Pharaoh's Dream (Genesis 41:17-24)

Image031 Joseph is Ruler Over All Egypt (Genesis 41:37-43)

Image032 Joseph Reveals Himself to His Brothers (Genesis 45:4-8)

The Twelve Tribes of Israel

Image033 Jacob Comes into Egypt (Genesis 46:5-7)

Ch3 Book of Exodus

(1 Kings 6:1)

I. Prologue (1-2)

Jacob's Descendants in Egypt

(Exodus 1:1-10)

(Exodus 17:14)

(Exodus 24:4)

Image034 The Discovery of Moses (Exodus 2:1-4)

II. God's Deliverance of Israel (3-18)

(Exodus 3:13-15) (Exodus 6:10-19)

Image035 Moses is Sent to Egypt (Exodus 3:7-10)

Ten Plagues of Egypt

(Exodus 7:20-21)

(Exodus 8:5-7)

(Exodus 8:12-13)

(Exodus 8:17-18)

(Exodus 9:1-4)

(Exodus 9:8-10)

(Exodus 9:15-18)

(Exodus 10:3-6)

(Exodus 10:21-23)

(Exodus 11:5-7)

Image036 The Origin of the Paschal Lamb (Exodus 12:21-23)

Image037 The Egyptians Drown in the Red Sea (Exodus 15:19-21)

Image038 God Gives Israel Bread/Water in Desert (Exodus 16:4-7)

III. Covenant at Sinai (19-24)

The Covenant of Moses

(Exodus 6:6)

(Exodus 15:13)

(Exodus 20:1-17)

(Exodus 20:22-24)

(Exodus 40:1-16)

Image039 Moses Receives God's Commandments (Exodus 20:1-6)

IV. God's Royal Tent in Israel (25-40)

Ark of the Covenant (Exodus 25:10-21)

Image040 The Idolatry of the Golden Calf (Exodus 32:1-5)

Image041 The Renewal of God's Covenant (Exodus 32:30-34)

(Exodus 34:27-35)

Temple History (I Kings 6:1-3)

Ch4 Book of Leviticus

(Leviticus 4:5-6)

I. The Five Main Offerings (1-7)

(Leviticus 1:3-4)

(Leviticus 2:4)

(Leviticus 4:2-3)

(Leviticus 5:16)

(Leviticus 7:5-6)

II. The Installation and Ministry of Aaron and His Sons (8-10)

(Leviticus 8:1-9)

III. The Distinction Between Clean and Unclean (11-15)

(Leviticus11:44)

(Leviticus 15:28-30)

IV. The Annual Day of Atonement (16)

Jewish Holidays

(Leviticus 16:17-22)

V. Holy Living (17-26)

Jewish Pilgrimage Festivals

(Leviticus 23:26-28)

VI. Regulations for Offerings Vowed to the Lord (27)

(Leviticus 27:1-8)

Ch5 Book of Numbers

(Numbers 1:1-3)

(Numbers 26:1-4)

I. At Sinai, Preparing to Depart for the Promised Land (1:1-10:10)

(Numbers 9:1-5)

II. The Journey from Sinai to Kadesh (10:11-12:16)

(Exodus 6:20)

(Numbers 12:10-14)

Image042 Spies are Sent into Canaan (Numbers 13:25-29)

III. Kadesh, the Delay Resulting from Rebellion (13:1-20:13)

(Numbers 20:1-6)

(Numbers 20:22-29)

IV. The Journey from Kadesh to the Plains of Moab (20:14-22:1)

(Numbers 21:10-20)

Image043 God Sends Fiery Serpents (Numbers 21:6-9)

V. Israel on Plains of Moab / Appendixes (22:2-36:13)

(Numbers 34:3-12)

Image044 The Appointment of Joshua (Numbers 27:15-21)

Ch6 Book of Deuteronomy

I. Preamble (1:1-5)

(Deuteronomy 1:1-5)

II. Historical Prologue (1:6-4:43)

(Deuteronomy 4:44-49)

Judaism Today

III. Stipulations of the Covenant (4:44-26:19)

(Deuteronomy 5:6-21)

IV. Ratification: Curses and Blessings (27-30)

(Deuteronomy 30:19-20)

V. Leadership Succession under the Covenant (31-34)

(Deuteronomy 33:6-25)

(Deuteronomy 17:18)

(Numbers 36:13)

(Deuteronomy 34:8-9)

(Joshua 1:1-2)

(Deuteronomy 28:1-6)

Authorship of the Pentateuch/Torah

(Joshua 1:7-8)

(1 Kings 2:3)

(Malachi 4:4)

(Mark 12:18-19)

(Acts 7:37-38)

(Acts 3:19-23)

Image045 The Death of Moses (Deuteronomy 33:1-5)

Deuteronomy Conclusion (Deuteronomy 34:1-12)

Resources:

{www.bible-history.com}

{www.biblehub.com}

{www.biblestudytools.com}

{www.catholicism.org}

{www.chabad.org}

{www.fivesolas.com}

{hirr.hartsem.edu/ency/index.html}

{www.iqrasense.com}

{www.jewishbrno.eu}

{www.jewishvirtuallibrary.org}

{www.pewresearch.org}

{www.religioustolerance.org}

{www.scofieldinstitute.org}

{www.usccb.org}

{www.wikipedia.org}

Bible Illustrations, (2003). Dover Publications.

Rose Book of Bible Charts, Maps, & Time Lines (2015). 3rd ed., Regent Publishing.

Cherry, Shai (2004). Introduction to Judaism, The Teaching Company.

Holland, Glen (2005). Religion in the Mediterranean World, The Teaching Company.

Levine, Amy-Jill (2001). The Old Testament, The Teaching Company.

Rendsburg, Gary (2010). The Dead Sea Scrolls, The Teaching Company.